Cambridge Elements ≡

Elements in Public Economics
edited by
Robin Boadway
Queen's University
Frank A. Cowell
The London School of Economics and Political Science
Massimo Florio
University of Milan

INEQUALITY AND OPTIMAL REDISTRIBUTION

Hannu Tanninen
University of Eastern Finland

Matti Tuomala
Tampere University

Elina Tuominen
Tampere University

CAMBRIDGE
UNIVERSITY PRESS

CAMBRIDGE
UNIVERSITY PRESS

University Printing House, Cambridge CB2 0DS, United Kingdom

One Liberty Plaza, 20th Floor, New York, NY 10006, USA

477 Williamstown Road, Port Melbourne, VIC 3207, Australia

314–321, 3rd Floor, Plot 3, Splendor Forum, Jasola District Centre,
New Delhi – 110025, India

79 Anson Road, #06–04/06, Singapore 079906

Cambridge University Press is part of the University of Cambridge.

It furthers the University's mission by disseminating knowledge in the pursuit of
education, learning, and research at the highest international levels of excellence.

www.cambridge.org
Information on this title: www.cambridge.org/9781108469111
DOI: 10.1017/9781108567503

First published 2019

A catalogue record for this publication is available from the British Library.

ISBN 978-1-108-46911-1 Paperback
ISSN 2516-2276 (online)
ISSN 2516-2268 (print)

Inequality and Optimal Redistribution

Elements in Public Economics

DOI: 10.1017/9781108567503
First published online: March 2019

Hannu Tanninen
University of Eastern Finland

Matti Tuomala
Tampere University

Elina Tuominen
Tampere University

Author for correspondence: Matti Tuomala, Matti.Tuomala@tuni.fi

Abstract: From the 1980s onwards income inequality has reversed course and increased in many advanced countries. Moreover, top income shares have increased, and top tax rates on upper-income earners have declined significantly in many Organisation for Economic Co-operation and Development (OECD) countries during this period. It is very difficult to account for the rise in income inequality using the standard labour supply/demand explanation. Hence, the role of redistributive taxation should not be dismissed in these discussions. Fiscal redistribution has become less effective in compensating for increasing inequalities since the 1990s. Some of the basic features of redistribution can be explained through the optimal tax framework developed by J. A. Mirrlees (1971). We survey some of the earlier results in linear and nonlinear taxation and produce some new numerical results both in the standard Mirrlees model and in its extensions. Given the key role of capital income in overall income inequality, we also consider the optimal taxation of capital income. We also examine empirically the relationship between the extent of redistribution and the components of the Mirrlees framework, including measures for inherent inequality and the government's redistributive preferences. We analyse briefly the redistributive role of factors such as publicly provided private goods, public employment, endogenous wages in the overlapping generations (OLG) model and income uncertainty that are missing in the standard model.

Keywords: inequality, redistribution, optimal taxation

ISBNs: 9781108469111 (PB), 9781108567503 (OC)
ISSNs: 2516-2276 (online), 2516-2268 (print)

Contents

1 Introduction

The post-war history of income inequality in advanced countries can be divided, at least roughly, into two phases. From 1945 to about the mid-1980s, pre-tax inequality decreased at least in part because of a reduction in skilled/unskilled wage differentials and asset inequality. The second phase occurred from the 1980s onwards, when inequality reversed course and increased. Using the Luxembourg Income Study (LIS) data, Immervoll and Richardson (2011) reported that in Organisation for Economic Co-operation and Development (OECD) countries, government redistribution has become less effective in compensating for increasing inequalities since the 1990s (see also Figure 1). Moreover, top income shares have increased in many advanced economies over the past three decades (see Figure 2),and top tax rates on upper-income earners have declined significantly in many OECD countries during this period (see Figure 3).

How can we explain this evolution of redistribution in OECD countries? For example, Atkinson, Piketty and Saez (2011) emphasised that it is very difficult to account for the rise in top incomes using the standard labour supply/demand explanation. Hence, the role of social policies and progressive taxation should not be dismissed in these discussions. In fact, some of the basic features of redistribution can be explained through the optimal tax framework developed by Mirrlees (1971). This model has dominated the economics of redistributive taxation for the past forty years. It captures the central features in thinking about the development of redistribution policy. Three elements of the model are useful for this purpose. First is the concept of inherent inequality. If there is no intervention by the government, inherent inequality will be fully reflected in disposable income. However, if the government wants to intervene – as seems to be the case in developed countries – we will find the second component of the Mirrlees model, the egalitarian objectives of the government. Moreover, if the government tries to redistribute income from high-income people to low-income people, there will be incentive and disincentive effects. In other words, the redistribution policy is the product of circumstances and objectives.

The recent optimal income tax literature has put a lot of emphasis on top marginal tax rates. As is well known, optimal income tax literature provides a striking result on a top marginal tax rate. The optimal marginal tax rate for the highest-wage person is zero. This result – due to Sadka (1976) – actually says that the highest income should be subject to a zero marginal tax rate. Strictly speaking, this result applies only to a single person at the very top of the income distribution, suggesting it is a mere theoretical curiosity. Moreover, it is unclear

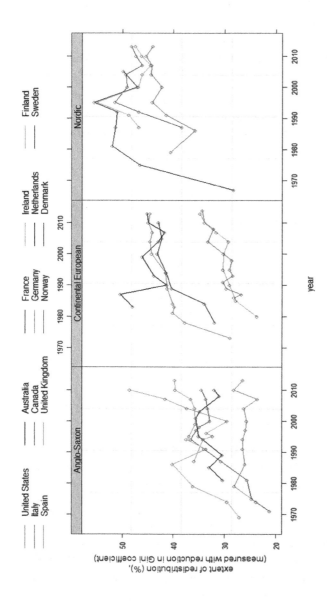

Figure 1 Evolution of the extent of redistribution measured with the relative reduction in the Gini coefficient in fourteen advanced countries (unbalanced data over the years 1967–2013). Authors' calculations from the LIS database

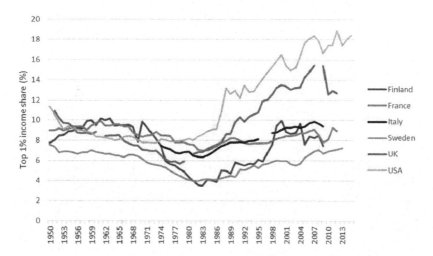

Figure 2 Evolution of the top 1 per cent pre-tax income shares in six countries. Data source: The World Inequality Database (formerly the World Wealth and Income Database, http://wid.world, accessed 1 April 2016)

that a 'top earner' even exists. For example, Saez (2001) argues that 'unbounded distributions are of much more interest than bounded distributions to address the high income optimal tax rate problem.' Without a top earner, the intuition for the zero top marginal rate does not apply, and marginal rates near the top of the income distribution may be positive and even large. Moreover, calculations in Tuomala (1984) show that the zero rate is not a good approximation for high incomes.

Notably, almost all analytical results focus on the structure of marginal tax rates to the neglect of average tax rates, which are arguably more important indicators of income tax progressivity.[1] Computational techniques can be utilised to say something about average rates. Moreover, the optimal tax structure is usually depicted in terms of skills rather than incomes, which is more relevant for actual policy recommendation. The derivation of optimal tax rates based on income is difficult, because the income of the tax function that is maximised is an endogenous variable depending on the tax function itself, so indirect effects have to be taken into account.

Starting around 1980, almost all developed countries have seen a sharp decline in tax progressivity. At the same time, many developed countries abolished annual or inherited wealth taxes. Moreover, a growing fraction of capital income was gradually left out of the income tax base. Consequently, only

---

[1] There are some exceptions; see Boadway and Jacquet (2008).

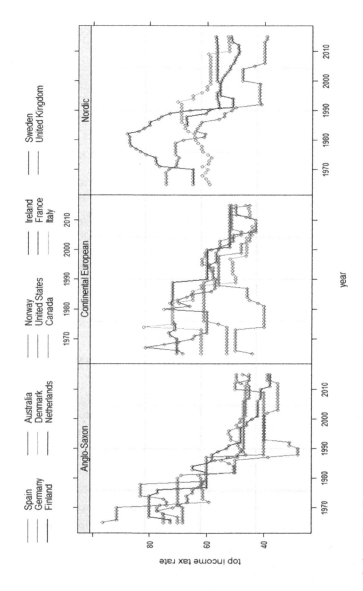

Figure 3 Evolution of top income tax rates in fourteen advanced countries over the years 1965–2015. Data sources: Piketty, Saez and Stantcheva (2014), OECD (2017) and the Association of Finnish Local and Regional Authorities (2017)

a labour income tax is any more progressive in the tax system. In the Nordic dual income tax system, this has been done explicitly. Dual income tax systems in turn have suffered from income shifting from progressively taxed labour income to capital income, which is taxed at a lower, flat rate.[2] We have also seen a rising share of capital in many advanced countries since the 1980s (see Piketty and Zucman, 2014). This, in turn, has increased overall income inequality because ownership of capital is much more unequally distributed than labour income. Therefore, equity considerations suggest capital income should be taxed more than labour income. If capital accumulation is sensitive to the net-of-tax return, these considerations in turn suggest going in a different direction. Moreover, capital is more mobile internationally than labour. Given these considerations, how should capital income be taxed? Roughly classifying, we can distinguish four alternatives to taxing capital income: not at all, linearly (Nordic dual income tax), relating the marginal tax rates of capital and labour incomes and taxing all income on the same schedule.

We survey some of the earlier results in linear and nonlinear taxation and produce some new numerical results both in the standard Mirrlees model and in its extensions. We consider how the optimal income tax schedule changes when income inequality, and in particular top income inequality, increases. We focus our attention both on the top tax rate (often thought of as the top marginal rates) and on the entire tax schedule. In particular, we consider how the optimal average tax schedule changes when top income inequality increases. Much of the discussion of optimal income taxation is about labour income. However, given the key role of capital income in overall income inequality, we also consider the optimal taxation of capital income, and in particular the taxation of top capital income.

We also examine empirically the relationship between the extent of redistribution and the elements of the Mirrlees model, including market income inequality, by utilising the LIS database and the government's redistributive preferences. The LIS database provides data on both factor and disposable incomes for a number of advanced countries over the past three to four decades, which facilitates the study of the extent of redistribution. In our empirical specifications, we study two alternative indicators to measure income inequality, namely the Gini coefficient and the percentile ratio (P90/P50). To measure the extent of redistribution, we use the relative reduction between the inequality indicator for factor incomes and disposable incomes. Previously, Tanninen and Tuomala (2005) examined the relationship between inherent inequality and the

---

[2] In Norway, for example, there is a progressive element in the capital income tax since shareholders pay a tax on what is defined as above-normal return on shares. Other capital income is taxed linearly. The Finnish dual income tax system is not purely linear anymore.

extent of redistribution by utilising the LIS data for a number of OECD countries over two to three decades. They found that redistribution in these countries is positively associated with inherent inequality until the mid-1990s. However, their empirical results were based on the assumption that the degree of espoused egalitarianism has remained constant over the period considered. There is now some recent individual-country evidence that there could have been a shift in norms, causing governments to become less willing to finance transfers and to levy progressive taxes, leading to reductions in the extent of redistribution. One could argue, in line with Atkinson (1999), that these kinds of changes have been episodic rather than time-trend, and are therefore rather difficult to justify, for example, in the context of median voter models. Thus, we focus here also on the role of the egalitarian objectives of government, which is an important component of the optimal income tax model. We construct our redistributive preference measure using the optimal top tax formula (for given labour supply elasticity) for which we have collected data from various sources.

The remainder of this Element is organised as follows. Section 2 analyses optimal linear income with different social objectives when inequality varies. Section 3 sets up the basic Mirrlees (1971) model and highlights the role of different elements of the model in determining the optimal redistribution. Section 4 analyses top marginal tax rates in the case of quasi-linear prefer-ences, Pareto-distributed skills and constant labour supply elasticities. We also study how elements left out of the standard model change top tax rates. Using numerical simulations, we study in Section 5 the role of different social objectives when inherent (or pre-tax inequality) income inequality increases. Section 6 analyses separable taxes on labour income and capital income in the simplified framework. Moreover, we briefly outline the case of optimal com-prehensive income tax. Section 7 examines empirically the relationship between the extent of redistribution and the components of the optimal non-linear tax model. In Section 8, we extend nonlinear taxation with the Veblen effect and analyse briefly the redistributive role of factors such as publicly provided private goods (health, education, social services), public employ-ment, endogenous wages in the overlapping generations (OLG) model and income uncertainty that are missing in the standard model. Section 9 concludes.

2 Optimal Linear Labour Income Taxation

We start by studying optimal linear taxes. In the linear income tax system, the tax is characterised by a lump sum income or a basic income B paid to each

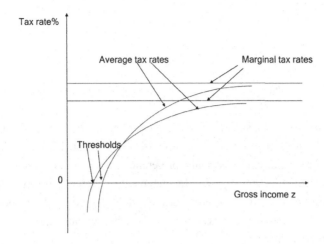

Figure 4 Marginal and average tax rates and linear income taxation

individual and a proportional tax on each euro earned at a rate t (the flat rate). If $t > 0$ and $B > 0$, the linear income tax is progressive in the sense that the average tax rate rises over the entire income range (see Figure 4). The linear income tax schedule provides a minimum guaranteed income to individuals whose income falls short of the critical level. This is the feature of the linear income tax system which leads us to refer to the section of the tax schedule below some gross income level z* in Figure 4 as a negative income tax.[3] The negative income tax system, basic income or the social dividend system has been proposed, supported and widely discussed by several distinguished economists such as James Meade, Milton Friedman, James Tobin and Tony Atkinson.[4] In particular, in a developing country context, linear income taxation can be justified as an easily implementable instrument.

Individuals face a linear income tax schedule $T(z) = -B + tz$. Every individual in this model faces a budget constraint $x(n) = (1 - t)z(n) + B$, where $(1 - t)$ is the net of tax rate, l is labour supply (l could be interpreted as the number of hours worked by the individual or equally well as effort), $z = nl$ is before-tax income. The revenue requirement of the government, R, to be used for expenditure on public goods, is taken as given. The government's budget constraint is:

---

[3] There is an interesting simpler extension of the linear income tax: a two-bracket income tax. It applies a constant rate t_1 to all income up to some specified level z* and another constant rate t_2 to all income over the specified level z*. See Slemrod et al. (1994), Apps et al. (2013).

[4] For some history on negative income tax and related proposals, see Kesselman and Garfinkel (1978).

$$\int_{0}^{\infty}[-B + tnl(1 - t, B)]f(n)dn = R, \tag{1}$$

where $Z = \int_{0}^{\infty} nlf(n)dn$ is the aggregate labour supply or income supply from the population.

The central issue considered in the analysis of the optimal linear income tax is that of choosing between the basic income and the associated tax rate. Therefore it is plausible to express individuals' preferences in terms of the indirect utility function, denoted $V(n(1 - t), B)$. In making this choice, the government is assumed to be constrained by a government budget and by the responses of taxpayers. The taxpayers are assumed to adjust their labour supply in response to changes in taxation.

In a typical optimal tax analysis, the objective for policy is to maximise social welfare, an object that is calculated through a social welfare function (SWF) that depends only upon the welfare levels of the individuals in society. The government has redistributive objectives represented by $W(V^1, \ldots, V^N)$ with $W' > 0$, $W'' < 0$. This is called prioritarianism by philosopher Derek Parfit (1991) (see also Matthew Adler, 2012). The idea of prioritarianism is that just distributions require giving greater weight, or priority, to individuals who are worse off. In fact, optimal tax theory has long made use of prioritarianism. In the founding paper of the modern optimal tax literature Mirrlees (1971) specified an objective for tax policy that directly translated the core idea of prioritarianism into his model's formal mathematical language.

The government's problem is to choose B and t so as to maximise the SWF:

$$\int_{0}^{\infty} W(V(n(1 - t), B))f(n)dn \tag{2}$$

under the budget constraint (1).

From the first-order condition of this problem we arrive at the condition (see the derivation in Tuomala (1985, 2016)

$$\frac{t}{1 - t} = \frac{1}{E}[1 - \frac{z(\psi)}{\bar{z}}], \tag{3}$$

where $E = \frac{d\bar{z}(1-t)}{d(1-t)\bar{z}}$ (the elasticity of earnings with respect $1 - t$, net-of-tax and averaging over the taxpayers must give $\bar{z} = \bar{z}(1 - t, B)$), $\psi = W_V V_B$ is the social marginal utility of income and $z(\psi) = \int_{0}^{\infty} \psi z f(n)dn / \int_{0}^{\infty} \psi f(n)dn$.

To illustrate the formula in (3) further, we have to specify the key elements of the model. We concentrate on the special case where there are no income effects on labour supply and the elasticity of labour supply with respect to the net-of-tax wage rate is constant. If ε denotes this elasticity, the quasi-linear indirect utility function is given by:

$$V(n(1-t),B) = B + \frac{[n(1-t)]^{1+\varepsilon}}{1+\varepsilon} \tag{4}$$

To simplify, we assume that the social marginal valuation depends only on wage (ability or productivity) n and not on the level of utility. We adopt a constant relative inequality aversion form of the welfare function. It is also called the Atkinson social welfare function by Adler (2012). The contribution to social welfare of the individual is $\frac{n^{1-\gamma}}{1-\gamma}$, where γ is the constant relative inequality aversion coefficient. In other words, the SWF is a quasi-concave function of n. Hence the social marginal value of income to an individual with wage rate n is proportional to $n^{-\gamma}$. It gives us the utilitarian case, where $\gamma = 0$, since we are back with the sum. Utilitarianism gives no value to equality in the distribution of well-being. It cares only about the total of well-being, not about how well-being is spread amongst the people. Rawls' formulation of the objective may be seen as a limiting case of the iso-elastic function as γ tends to infinity. Hence W takes the form min u, i.e. maximin. Rawls (1974) objects to this interpretation. For him, it is wrong to suggest that we can 'shift smoothly from the moral conception to another simply by varying the parameter' (γ). (Rawls, 1974, p. 664). Rawls (1974) suggests that the important feature of a distributive criterion is that it should serve as a public principle. He says that 'citizens generally should be able to understand it and have some confidence that it is realized' (Rawls, 1974, p. 143). He claims that the maximin, unlike utilitarianism, satisfies this criterion of sharpness or transparency. Hence, a change in tax policy that benefits the least advantaged should be easily observable.

The key axiomatic difference between utilitarianism and prioritarianism is the *Pigou-Dalton axiom* (axiom of transfers), here understood in terms of well-being. With $\gamma = 0$, the SWF is no longer prioritarian. Pigou-Dalton is not satisfied.[5]

Next we turn to the distribution of n. The excellent Pareto fit of the top tail of the distribution has been well known for more than a century, since the pioneering work of Pareto (1896), and has been verified in many countries and many

---

[5] Pigou-Dalton: A gap-diminishing transfer of well-being from someone better off to someone worse off, leaving everyone else unaffected, is an ethical improvement.

periods, as summarised in Atkinson et al. (2011). In those twenty-four countries reported in Atkinson et al. (2011), the Pareto parameter typically varies between 3.0 and 1.67. The top tail of the income distribution is closely approximated by a Pareto distribution.[6] The higher α (i.e. lower coefficient $\alpha/(\alpha-1)$; i.e. less fat upper tail) implies lower inequality. A lower coefficient means larger top income shares and higher income inequality. In Finland during the period 1990–2014, the Pareto parameter (taxable income) varied between 3.7 (1992) and 1.79 (2004) (see Figure 13 in Section 6).

We assume here that the n-distribution is an unbounded Pareto distribution $f(n) = \frac{1}{n^{1+a}}$ for a > 0, i.e. a Pareto tail with the coefficient α. Thus, the right tail is thicker as α is smaller, implying that only low-order moments exist. The Pareto parameter in itself is an appropriate measure for increasing top income shares. Using the property of the Pareto distribution $E(n^j) = \frac{a n_0^j}{\alpha - j}$, we can calculate the values of the optimal tax rate and of the basic income from the following formula:

$$\frac{t}{1-t} = \frac{1}{\varepsilon}[1 - M] \tag{5}$$

where $M = \left\{ \frac{\left[\frac{1-\frac{1+\varepsilon}{a}}{1}\right]}{\left[\frac{1-\frac{1+\varepsilon}{a+\gamma}}{1}\right]} \right\}$

Substituting the labour supply function $l = [n(1-t)]^\varepsilon$ for the revenue constraint, we can express the basic income and the revenue relative to the average earnings (denoted by b and r, respectively). We rewrite the revenue constrains as follows: $b = t(1-t)^\varepsilon - r$. The results are presented in Table 1. The revenue requirement is set to zero, thus the system is purely redistributive. Results are shown for two different values of labour supply elasticity and for two different values regarding income dispersion, $\alpha = 2$ and $\alpha = 2.5$. The tax rates are high for all the combinations of parameter values.

Most work on optimal nonlinear and linear income taxation used the lognormal distribution to describe the distribution of productivities $ln(n; m, \sigma^2)$ with support $[0,\infty)$ with parameters m and σ (see Aitchison and Brown, 1957). The first parameter, m, is log of the median and the second parameter is the variance of log wage. The latter one is itself an inequality measure. Using the property of the lognormal distribution $\ln E(n^j) = jm + j^2\sigma^2/2$, we can obtain the optimal tax rate formula $\frac{t}{1-t} = \frac{1}{\varepsilon}[1 - e^{-\gamma(1+\varepsilon)\sigma^2}]$ or using the property of lognormal

---

[6] It is still the case that the original purpose of the Pareto function is its most fruitful application. This view is nicely expressed by Cowell (1977) when he writes that: 'Although the Pareto formulation has proved to be extremely versatile in the social sciences, in my view the purpose for which it was originally employed is still its most useful application – an approximate description of the distribution of income and wealth among the rich and the moderately rich.'

Table 1 Tax rates t and b: Pareto distribution, $\alpha = 2.0$, $r = 0.0$

ε	$\gamma = 1.0$	$\gamma = 1.0$	$\gamma = 2.0$	$\gamma = 2.0$
	t	b	t	b
0.25	58.8	51.5	64.0	57.0
0.5	50.0	35.4	54.5	46.8

Tax rates t and b: Pareto distribution, $\alpha = 2.5$, $r = 0.0$

ε	$\gamma = 1.0$	$\gamma = 1.0$	$\gamma = 2.0$	$\gamma = 2.0$
	t	b	t	b
0.25	46.8	40.0	55.3	45.0
0.5	38.0	30.0	44.0	33.0

Table 2 Tax rates t: Lognormal distribution, $r = 0.0$, $\sigma = 0.7$

ε	$\gamma = 1$	$\gamma = 1$	$\gamma = 2.0$	$\gamma = 2.0$
	t	b	t	b
0.25	57.7	46.5	69.4	51.6
0.5	44.1	33.0	55.9	37.0

Tax rates t: Lognormal distribution, $r = 0.0$, $\sigma = 1.0$

e	$\gamma = 1$	$\gamma = 1$	$\gamma = 2.0$	$\gamma = 2.0$
	t	b	t	b
0.25	64.8	50.0	73.9	52.8
0.5	51.2	35.8	60.7	38.0

distribution that $\ln(1 + cv^2) = \sigma^2$, where cv is the coefficient of variation, we can rewrite:

$$t = \frac{1}{1 + \varepsilon/[1 + cv^2]^{-\gamma(1+\varepsilon)}}. \tag{6}$$

A wide range of values for the parameter γ have been employed in the literature, varying typically from 0.5 to 2.0. Results are shown in Table 2 for two different values of labour supply elasticity, for two different values regarding income dispersion and for four different values of inequality aversion. Our numerical examples tend to suggest that both the tax rates and lump sum incomes increase when pre-tax inequality increases. This in turn implies that average tax rates increase. Figure 4 illustrates this change.

Table 3 Tax rates t: Lognormal distribution, r = 0.0. F(n*) is the number of people below the poverty line.

	F(n*) = 0.3	F(n*) = 0.3	F(n*) = 0.3	F(n*) = 0.3	F(n*) = 0.4	F(n*) = 0.4	F(n*) = 0.4	F(n*) = 0.4
e	$\sigma = 1.0$	$\sigma = 1.0$	$\sigma = 0.7$	$\sigma = 0.7$	$\sigma = 1.0$	$\sigma = 1.0$	$\sigma = 0.7$	$\sigma = 0.7$
	t	b	t	b	t	b	t	b
0.25	79.0	53.4	78.0	53.4	78.0	53.4	77.0	53.0
0.5	66.0	38.5	65.0	38.4	64.0	38.0	63.0	38.3

Following Kanbur, Paukkeri, Pirttilä and Tuomala (2018), we next compare our results in Table 2 with the case when the government's aim is to minimise poverty (see Table 3). We have the same instruments, t and b, that are used not for welfare maximisation but for poverty minimisation. As in Kanbur et al. (2018), we take a poverty index of the form developed by Foster, Greer and Thorbecke (1984).[7] They have proposed defining a poverty index as the average of these poverty gaps raised to some power χ across individuals. When $\chi = 1$, it is just the proportion of units below the poverty line multiplied by the average poverty gap. Again, we concentrate on the special case where there are no income effects on labour supply and the elasticity of labour supply with respect to the net-of-tax wage rate is constant. Typically, poverty indices consist of computing some average measure of deprivation by setting individual needs as defined earlier at the agreed-upon poverty line.

The results shown in the tables illustrate clearly that at conventional inequality aversion levels, optimal welfaristic tax rates lie well below the poverty-minimising rates. Only as inequality aversion becomes extremely high do the welfaristic rates approach the poverty-minimising ones. With poverty minimisation as the social objective, optimal tax rates are close to the revenue-maximising 'maximin' rate.

Another comparison could be the results of Stern (1976), who ended up with a tax rate of 43 per cent when the elasticity of substitution between consumption and leisure is 0.5. The numerical examples in Tables 1, 2 and 3 and in Stern's results tend to suggest that the tax rates for the poverty minimisation case are likely to be higher than for many welfarist (prioritarian) examples.

---

[7] $P_\gamma = \int_{\underline{n}}^{n^*} [\frac{x(n) - x^*}{x^*}]^\chi f(n) dn$ where x* is the poverty line.

Before moving to the general optimal nonlinear income tax problem, there is an interesting simpler extension of linear income tax: a two-bracket income tax. It applies a constant rate t_1 to all income up to some specified level z* and another constant rate t_2 to all income over the specified level z* (See Apps et al. 2013).

3 The Optimal Nonlinear Labour Income Tax

Next, we turn to nonlinear income taxation. For simplicity, we assume that the utility function is additive:

$$u = U(x) + V(1 - l) \tag{7}$$

defined over consumption x and hours worked l, with $U_x > 0$ and $V_l < 0$ (subscripts indicating partial derivatives). Individuals differ only in the pre-tax wage n they can earn. The aim of policy can be expressed as maximising the following social welfare criterion:

$$W = \int_0^\infty W(u(n))f(n)dn, \tag{8}$$

where W (.) is the social welfare criterion that takes individual utilities as its arguments. It is an increasing in each individual's utility, so that it fully embodies the Pareto principle. At the same time, it may incorporate aversion to inequality, or a degree of priority to the worse off. Prioritarianism appears to fit aptly into this formal structure, requiring only that the SWF be strictly concave in individual welfare levels, that is, for $u_j > u_i$, $W'(u_j) < W'(u_i)$. In words, the strict concavity of the SWF means that an additional unit of utility for an individual with a high level of utility increases social welfare by less than an additional unit of utility for an individual with low utility. The government cannot observe individuals' productivities or abilities and thus is restricted to setting taxes and transfers as a function only of earnings, $T(z(n))$, where $z = nl$. The government maximises (8) subject to the resource constraint or the revenue constraint:

$$\int_0^\infty (z - x)f(n)dn = R, \tag{9}$$

where R can be interpreted as the required revenue for essential public goods. The more non-tax revenue a government receives from external sources, the lower is R. In addition to the revenue constraint, the government faces incentive compatibility constraints. These in turn state that each n individual maximises utility by choice of hour or labour effort. Hence

$$u[nl - T(nl(n))] + V[1 \quad l(n)] \geq u[n'ln') - T(n'l(n'))] +$$
$$V[1 - n'l(n')/n)], \text{ for all n and } n'. \tag{10}$$

It means that an individual of type n has to work n'/n times that of type n' to get the same income. Following Mirrlees (1971) in the continuum case, it is useful to employ the following 'trick'. Totally differentiating utility with respect to n, and making use of workers' utility maximisation condition, i.e. each n individual chooses $x(n)$ and $z(n)$ to maximise utility subject to the constraint $c(z) = nl - T(nl)$, we obtain the following condition:

$$\frac{du}{dn} = \frac{-lV_l}{n}. \tag{11}$$

provided a single-crossing property[9] (or Mirrlees-Spence condition) holds for every n individual incentive compatibility is equivalent to two constraints, one that z is non-decreasing in n, and the condition (11).

In other words, the optimal income tax problem is that of finding a function $c(z) = nl - T(nl)$ that maximises (8) subject to the linearized resource constraint (9). Incorporating the resource constraint into the maximand (8), we have a control-theory problem to maximise:

$$\int_0^\infty [W + \lambda(nl - x))f(n)dn \tag{12}$$

where λ is the multiplier on the resource constraint, c is a function of u, z and n given by utility function (7) and subject to the differential equation (11). In addition, we assume that z is non-decreasing. The optimality conditions for this problem are obtained by treating u as a state variable and l as a control variable, and x is determined from the utility function.

Omitting details (see the derivation in Tuomala, 2016), from the first-order conditions of the government's maximisation, we obtain the condition for the

---

[8] The first-order condition of an individual's optimisation problem is only a necessary condition for the individual's choice to be optimal, but we assume here that it is sufficient as well. Assumptions that assure sufficiency are provided by Mirrlees (1976). Note also that while we here presume an internal solution for l, (11) remains valid even if individuals were bunched at $l = 0$ since, for them, du/dn = 0.

[9] It implies that indifference curves in consumption-gross income space become flatter the higher is an individual's wage rate, which in turn ensures that both consumption and gross earnings increase with the wage rate. Furthermore, a single crossing condition implies that for any income tax schedule, more able individuals choose to earn a higher income than less qualified individuals (if the marginal tax rate is less than 100 per cent).

optimal marginal tax rate. It is useful to write the ABC formula for marginal rates,[10] denoted by $t(z) = T'(z)$, in terms of traditional labour supply elasticities, E^u and E^c;[11,12,13].

$$\frac{t}{1-t} = \underbrace{\left[\frac{1+E^u}{E^c}\right]}_{A_n} \underbrace{\left[\frac{[1-F(n)]}{nf(n)}\right]}_{B_n} \underbrace{\left[\frac{U_x \int_n^\infty [1 - W'U_x^{(p)}/\lambda] f(p) dp}{(1-F(n))}\right]}_{C_n}, \quad (13)$$

where E^u is the uncompensated elasticity of labour supply and E^c in turn is the compensated elasticity.[14]

It should be clear from (13) that the variation of the optimal marginal tax rate with the level of income is a complex matter. Applying (13), it appears that four elements on the right-hand side of (13) determine optimum tax rates: labour supply elasticity (A) and income effects (A&C), the shape of the skill distribution (B&C) (B is the distribution ratio) and marginal social welfare weights (C).

To understand intuitively the marginal tax formula (13), we consider the following perturbation or tax reform: raise the marginal tax rate for individuals with income z' (say, in a small interval z' to z' + Δ where Δ is infinitesimal), leaving all other marginal tax rates unchanged. The perturbation has two effects. First, individuals with income levels in the treated interval will have their labour supply further distorted. The higher the marginal tax rate, the higher the distortion. Second, individuals with income levels above z' + Δ will pay higher taxes,

---

[10] There is an important difference between (13) and the formulation in Saez (2001, p. 215). Taking into account that the tax rules and other parameters will determine the relationship between the ability distribution and the resulting income distribution, Saez (2001) translates the results from ones in terms of the distribution of abilities to ones in terms of the distribution of income. In other words, Saez makes a step forward in deriving an optimal tax formula by expressing his optimal tax formula in terms of the notion of virtual earnings distribution and verifies the consistency of his solution to the Mirrlees one. Saez (2001, p. 215) defines the virtual density at earnings level z as 'the density of incomes that would take place at z if the tax schedule T (:) were replaced by the linear tax schedule tangent to T (:) at level z'.

[11] Revesz (1989), Atkinson (1995), Diamond (1998), Piketty (1997) and Saez (2001) formulated the Mirrlees first-order condition in terms of elasticities. See also Wilson (1993) in the context of nonlinear pricing.

[12] Note: $\frac{t}{1-t} = \frac{1}{1-t} - 1 = \frac{U_x n}{V_l} - 1$.

[13] The marginal tax rate in formula (18) is depicted as $\frac{t}{1-t}$ instead of t. The reason is that the tax here is applied to the tax-inclusive tax base or after-tax income.

[14] Differentiating the first order condition of the individual maximisation, $U_x n(1-t) + V_l = 0$, with respect to net wage, labour supply and virtual income, b, we have after some manipulation elasticity formulas: $E^u = \frac{(V_l/l) - (V_l/U_x)^2 U_{xx}}{V_{ll} + (V_l/U_x)^2 U_{xx}}$, (income effect parameter) $I = \frac{-(V_l/U_x)^2 U_{xx}}{V_{ll} + (V_l/U_x)^2 U_{xx}}$ and, from the Slutsky equation, $E^c = E^u - I$, then $E^c = \frac{(V_l/y)}{V_{ll} + (V_l/U_x)^2 U_{xx}}$.

but they will face no additional distortion because their marginal tax rates are the same. That is, the higher marginal rate at z' is inframarginal for them. The first effect is a cost and the second effect is a benefit because the SWF values redistribution. Roughly speaking, the higher the benefit is from the second effect relative to the cost of the first effect, the higher should be the marginal tax rate at z'. The formula for the optimal marginal tax rates reflects this logic. The higher the ratio $\frac{(1-F(n))}{nf(n)}$ the higher is the benefit relative to the cost because the distorted group is smaller relative to the group who pays more taxes. The smaller the labour supply elasticity the lower is the cost, because the lower is the distortion. The higher is $1 - \frac{W'U_x}{\lambda}$, the higher is the benefit because the average value of $W'U_x$ on the interval $[n, \infty)$ is lower.

But (13) is still too complex, with a number of different influences in play, to allow useful interpretation. Therefore, following the lead of Mirrlees (1971), numerical simulations have proved useful in generating useful results.[15] Before going to numerical simulations we analyse top marginal tax rates.

4 Optimal Top Marginal Rates and Quasi-Linear Preferences in Consumption

For simplicity, we concentrate on the special case where preferences are quasi-linear in consumption (as earlier in linear income taxation). There are no income effects in labour supply. This special case is extensively used in both theoretical and applied optimal tax literature. The quasi-linear assumption is also restrictive because it eliminates declining marginal utility of consumption (utility is linear in x), which is a key motivation for redistribution. Preferences are represented by a utility function:

$$u = x + V(1 - l). \tag{14}$$

Now $U_x = 1$. Equation (14) with $V = 1 - \frac{l^{1+\frac{1}{\varepsilon}}}{1+\frac{1}{\varepsilon}}$ implies a labour supply function $l = ((1 - t)n)^{\varepsilon}$ with a constant elasticity ε.[16] The optimal marginal tax formula takes now the following form:

$$\frac{t}{1-t} = \underbrace{\left[1 + \frac{1}{\varepsilon}\right]}_{A_n} \underbrace{\left[\frac{[1 - F(n)]}{nf(n)}\right]}_{B_n} \underbrace{\left[\frac{\int\limits_{n}^{\infty}[1 - \varphi]f(p)dp}{(1 - F(n))}\right]}_{C_n}. \tag{15}$$

---

[15] Tuomala (2016) gives details of the computational procedure.
[16] With these preferences, we note from the first-order condition, $[((1 - t)n]^{\varepsilon}$, that everybody with n > 0 works.

With quasi-linear preferences in consumption, we define the marginal social welfare weight on taxpayer n as $\varphi(n) = \frac{W'(u)}{\lambda}$, where $\lambda = \int_0^\infty W'[u(x)]f(p)dp$[17].

Hence, $\varphi(n) = \frac{W'(u)}{\lambda}$ average to one. In words, the welfare weights $\varphi(n)$ measure the social value of giving a unit of income to an individual with ability n, relative to the social value of dividing it equally among all individuals. In the classical utilitarian case, φ is constant for all n, and hence by the end-point condition is equal to 1. Then the marginal tax rates are uniformly zero. There is complete distributional indifference (given the quasi-linearity in preferences). There is no taxation.

If there is no upper bound of the skill distribution, the marginal tax rate at the top is not any more zero. Now we make an empirically plausible assumption that there is no upper bound. For any SWF W with a property that $\lim_{u \to \infty} W'(u) = 0$, and individual preferences represented by (14), then the integral in (15) asymptotically converges to 1 and $\frac{t(n)}{1-t(n)}$ converges to $\frac{t(n)}{1-t(n)} = \left[1 + \frac{1}{\varepsilon}\right]\frac{1-F(n)}{nf(n)}$ from below. In the case of the unbounded Pareto distribution of skills above the modal skill $\frac{1-F(n)}{nf(n)} = \frac{1}{a}$, the asymptotic optimal marginal tax rate is given by $\lim_{n \to \infty} \frac{t(n)}{1-t(n)} = \left[1 + \frac{1}{\varepsilon}\right]\frac{1}{a}$, where a is the Pareto coefficient. Hence

$$t = \frac{1}{1 + a/\xi}, \tag{16}$$

where $\xi = \left[1 + \frac{1}{\varepsilon}\right]$. Formula (16) is an explicit formula for the optimal top income tax rate. It is also the asymptotic optimal marginal tax rate coming out of the standard nonlinear optimal tax model of Mirrlees (1971). That is, the optimal marginal tax rate is approximately the same over the range of very high incomes where the distribution is Pareto and the SWF has curvature so that $W'[u(n)]$ tends to zero when u tends to infinity.[18] Assuming that the average marginal social welfare weight among top-bracket income earners is zero allows us to obtain an upper bound on the optimal top tax rate. Hence (16) gives revenue maximising and the Rawlsian[19,20] tax rate.

---

[17] If the minimum income is zero, then this is not true.

[18] See also Dahan and Strawczynzki (2012).

[19] Maximising the utility of the worst-off person in society is not the original version of Rawls (1971). It is a kind of welfarist version. 'To interpret the difference principle as the principle of maximin utility (the principle to maximize the well-being of the least advantaged person) is a serious misunderstanding from a philosophical standpoint' (Rawls, 1982).

[20] In maximin case, in (13) C is $\int (f(p)/U_x)dp$. It is declining with n since u(x) is concave and the integral term declines in n. This might suggest declining marginal rates.

We employ the property of (16) to calculate optimal top income tax rates using reduced-form estimates of the labour supply elasticity for top incomes and a Pareto parameter from the income distribution. It means that we have to focus on both elasticity and income distribution.

One may argue that it is too extreme to put zero asymptotic welfare weight at the top earners. For example, Feldstein (2012) argues that it is repugnant to set weights in this way. Alternatively, we might assume that φ has a positive lower bound which is approached as n rises without limit. Of course it is not obvious how to determine a positive lower bound. Given the lower point of φ the optimal rate is now:

$$t = \frac{1 - \varphi}{1 - \varphi + \varepsilon\alpha} \tag{17.}$$

The optimal top marginal tax rate is decreasing with the elasticity ε and the social marginal welfare weight on the top earner φ and increasing in the Pareto parameter α. This rate is also less than the revenue-maximising rate with the same Pareto parameter and elasticity.

Atkinson (1990) considers the case of the charitable conservative position, where the marginal welfare weight of consumption takes on two values – a high one for poor people and a low one for non-poor people. The weights characterising charitable conservatism as specified by Atkinson (1990) fall discontinuously at the poverty line, n_{pov}, and are constant thereafter at a positive level. The government is concerned with the bottom N_{pov} of the population, giving them a weight $\frac{\varphi_c}{\kappa}$ and φ_c for the rest of the population. Figure 5 illustrates the pattern of the weights. If we take a charitable conservative position, the last term in (15) is equal to $(1 - \varphi_c)$. On average the social marginal valuation of consumption equal to 1 implies:

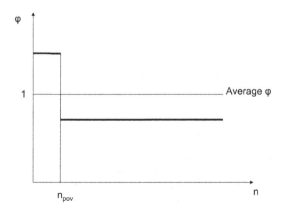

Figure 5 Charitable conservatism

Table 4 Prioritarian top marginal tax rates (%), $\varphi = 1/3$ [21]

	$\alpha = 1.5$	$\alpha = 2.0$	$\alpha = 3.0$
$\varepsilon = 0.25$	64.1	57.3	47.2
$\varepsilon = 0.50$	47.2	40.1	30.9

Revenue-maximising ('Rawlsian') top marginal tax rates (%), $\varphi = 0.0$

	$\alpha = 1.5$	$\alpha = 2.0$	$\alpha = 3.0$
$\varepsilon = 0.25$	72.7	66.7	57.1
$\varepsilon = 0.50$	57.1	50.0	40.0

Charitable conservatism top marginal tax rates (%), $\kappa = 0.25$

	$\alpha = 1.5$	$\alpha = 2.0$	$\alpha = 3.0$
$\varepsilon = 0.25$	52.0	44.0	35.0
$\varepsilon = 0.50$	35.0	32.0	21.0

$$(1 - N_{pov})\varphi_c + N_{pov}\frac{\varphi_c}{\kappa} = 1, \tag{18}$$

where N_{pov} is a fraction of people who are below the poverty line. It can be calculated when we know κ and N_{pov}.

$$\frac{t}{1-t} = \left[1 + \frac{1}{\varepsilon}\right]\frac{(1 - \varphi_c)}{a}. \tag{19}$$

Table 4 illustrates with some parameter values top marginal rates with different social objectives (prioritarian, revenue maximising [Rawlsian] and charitable conservatism). As we mentioned in the introduction, since the end of the 1970s, top tax rates on upper-income earners have declined significantly in many OECD countries, again mainly in English-speaking countries. For example, the US top marginal federal individual tax rate was a remarkably high 91 per cent in the 1950s–1960s, but is only 35 per cent nowadays. In other advanced countries e.g. in Nordic countries, top tax rates on upper-income earners have declined dramatically since the beginning of the 1990s. The top tax rate in Finland was 44.3 per cent in 2010. The corresponding top tax rate was 62.7 per cent in 1990.

Earlier in this Element, we provided some answers based on the standard model. How to assess these results for the top marginal tax rate? It is clear that it

---

[21] For example, in Finland and Sweden, φ has been around one third over the past decades. See our estimates for fourteen countries in Figure C1.

depends on whether elements left out of the standard model change them. What is missing from the analysis presented earlier?

Reference incomes: Bockin and Sheshinski (1978), Oswald (1983) and Tuomala (1990), for example, consider the implication of utility interdependence (or 'envy') – the situation in which individuals' utility is negatively affected by others' income – on optimal income taxation. There is nowadays ample evidence that people indeed care about their relative positions (see e.g. Blanchflower and Oswald, 2004).

Kanbur and Tuomala (2013) constructed a comparison consumption level to take account of externality effect be as follows:

$$\zeta = \int \pi(n)x(n)f(n)dn \tag{20}$$

There are a number of alternative interpretations of the variable ζ. The simplest one is obtained if each of the π weights is equal to 1. In this case, the average consumption is the comparison consumption level. We can choose the weights ω so that ζ is the consumption of the richest individual (this corresponds to Veblen's idea), of the median individual or of something in between the richest and the median. It is difficult to say without empirical evidence which is the most plausible interpretation. Here we restrict attention to the case where $\pi = 1$ for all n so that ζ is the average consumption of people in the economy, $\bar{x}$. Otherwise the model in Kanbur and Tuomala (2013) is similar to Mirrlees (1971).

The utilitarian case: We assume the utility function is $u = x - v\bar{x} - l^{1+\frac{1}{\varepsilon}}$, i.e., quasi-linear in consumption and constant labour supply elasticity ε, quasi-linear preferences with $U_x = 1$ and further if the n-distribution is a Pareto distribution. If $W'[u(n)]$ goes to zero as n rises, then for sufficiently large n, $t/(1-t)$ is increasing and converges to $\frac{\varsigma}{\lambda}(1 + \frac{1+\varepsilon}{a}) + \frac{1+\varepsilon}{a}$ (where λ is the multiplier of the government budget constraint and ς is the multiplier of a comparison consumption level). Thus, the marginal tax rate t increases with n and converges to a positive limit. Hence the result shown by Diamond (1998) without relative consumption concern also holds here. Note that the positive limit increases with the scope of relativity ς and α^{-1} (i.e. with increasing inequality). To get a better understanding quantitatively, we calculate an example. Assume an elasticity of 0.3; the social marginal welfare weight at the top decile is 0.5, where $\frac{(1-F(n))}{nf(n)} = 0.5$ and $v = 1/2$. The optimal marginal tax rate at this income level is 75 per cent; without any relative consumption concern it would be 50 per cent. Clearly, the impact of relativity on the marginal tax rate is quantitatively significant. There may also be some interest in noting that when W' = 1, i.e., there is complete

Table 5 Rawlsian top marginal tax rates (%) when people care about relative consumption

Relative concern	$\epsilon = 1/3$ $\alpha = 2.0$	$\epsilon = 1/3$ $\alpha = 3.0$	$\epsilon = 1/2$ $\alpha = 2.0$	$\epsilon = 1/2$ $\alpha = 3.0$	$\epsilon = 1$ $\alpha = 2.0$	$\epsilon = 1$ $\alpha = 3.0$
$v = 0$	66.6	57.0	60.0	50.0	50.0	40.0
$v = 1/2$	83.3	78.6	80.0	75.0	75.0	70.0

distributional indifference (given the quasi-linearity in preferences), then all taxation must be Pigouvian. Without relativity concern ($v = 0$), the optimal income tax is simply the Mirrleesian tax.

The Rawlsian case: If we assume the Rawlsian social objective of maximising the utility of the worst-off person in society, and if the upper part of the n-distribution is the unbounded Pareto distribution and the utility function is quasi-linear in consumption, we have:

$$\frac{t}{1-t} = \phi + \left[1 + \frac{1}{\varepsilon}\right] \frac{1}{a} [1 + \phi], \tag{21}$$

where $\phi = \frac{v}{1-v}$.

Table 5 illustrates and presents the marginal tax rates for different parameter values, when $\alpha = 2$ and 3, $v = 0$ and 1/2 and $\epsilon = 1/3$, 1/2 and 1. It shows how the top marginal tax rate decreases when the elasticity of labour supply ϵ increases, the Pareto parameter α increases and the degree of relative consumption concern declines. If the whole distribution of wages is an unbounded Pareto distribution, then optimal marginal tax rates are constant and positive.

Top income earners and the labour market: There are good reasons to suspect that top income earners are not paid their marginal product. For example, Persson and Sandmo (2005) argue that a 'tournament' model where wages are determined not by productivity but by one's productivity relative to other workers would be more relevant to the salaries of top executives. It may therefore be a more suitable framework within which to examine the optimal top tax rate than the standard one.

Socially unproductive rent-seeking: If the economic activity at high incomes is primarily socially unproductive rent-seeking, then it would be plausible to impose higher marginal rates at top income levels than those calculated earlier. Based on the rent-seeking by executives, and how cutting top rates of tax encouraged this rent-seeking, Piketty, Saez and Stantcheva (2014) provide an alternative model that they call a 'compensation bargaining' model. Piketty et al. argue that with lower tax rates, the CEO has a much greater incentive to put lots of effort into the bargaining process with the company.

CEOs, rather than the tax authority, will receive the rewards from being successful. As mentioned earlier, Piketty et al. show a 'clear correlation between the drop in top marginal tax rates and the surge in top income shares'. Furthermore, they have microeconomic evidence that CEOs' pay for firms' performance (such as stock options) that is outside the CEOs' control is more important when tax rates are low. Lockwood, Nathanson and Weyl (2012) in turn argue that: 'If higher-paying professions (e.g. finance and management) generate less positive net externalities than lower-paying professions (e.g. public service and education) taxation may enhance efficiency.' Rothschild and Scheuer (2014) in turn analyse rent-seeking externalities with two professions or sectors: one with negative rent-seeking externalities, and the other with none.

What are the tax policy implications of top tax rates based on the formula with rent-seeking activities? They simply reflect weaknesses of the tax system or more generally social and economic institutions. In other words, what fraction of the rent-seeking activities can be eliminated by better institutions?

5 Numerical Optimal Nonlinear Tax Schedules

We have to specify four key elements in the optimal nonlinear income tax model in order to solve it numerically. Next, we consider each of them in turn.

The first factor is the distribution of income-earning abilities. Following Mirrlees (1971), most of the work on optimal nonlinear and linear income taxation used the lognormal distribution[22] to describe the distribution of productivities (e.g. Atkinson, 1973; Stern, 1976; Tuomala, 1984, 1990; Kanbur and Tuomala, 1994; Immonen, Kanbur, Keen and Tuomala, 1998, 2009; Mankiw, Weinzierl and Yagan, 2009). As is commonly known, the lognormal distribution fits reasonably well over a large part of the income range, but not so well at the upper tail. The Pareto distribution in turn fits well at the upper tail. Champernowne (1952)[23] proposes a model in which individual incomes are assumed to follow a random walk in the logarithmic scale. Here we use the two-parameter version of the Champernowne distribution (also known as the Fisk distribution).[24] This distribution approaches asymptotically a form of Pareto

---

[22] $ln(n; m, \sigma^2)$ with support $[0, \infty)$ with parameters m and σ (see Aitchison and Brown, 1957). The first parameter m is log of the median and the second parameter is the variance of log wage. The latter one is itself an inequality measure.

[23] In fact, the distribution had been introduced much earlier by Champernowne (1937), but that work is even less well known.

[24] See Champernowne and Cowell (1999).

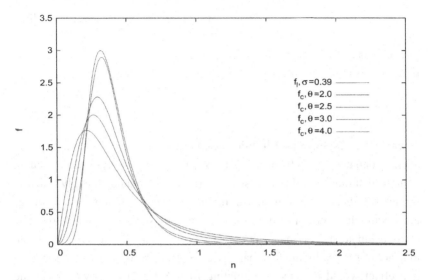

Figure 6 f_c = Champernowne distribution, f_l = lognormal distribution, $m = e^{-1}$

distribution for large values of wages, but it also has an interior maximum. As the lognormal, the Champernowne distribution exhibits the following features: asymmetry, a left humpback and a long right-hand tail. It has a thicker upper tail than in the lognormal case. Among two parameter distributions, the Champernowne with parameters m (scale parameter)[25] and θ (shape parameter) is the best fit for pre-tax income distribution in Finland (1990–2010) (Figure 6). The θ parameter varies from 2.78 to 2.4. Over the period from the latter part of the 1990s to 2010, the θ parameter was almost constant, being around 2.5. A low range estimate, say $\theta = 2$, reflects high inequality, and $\theta = 3$ in turn a high range estimate (low inequality).

The probability density function and the cumulative distribution function of the Champernowne distribution are:

$$f(n) = \theta\left(\frac{m^{\theta} n^{\theta-1}}{(m^{\theta} + n^{\theta})^2}\right) \quad F(n) = 1 - \frac{m^{\theta}}{(m^{\theta} + n^{\theta})} \tag{22}$$

where θ is a shape parameter and m is a scale parameter. For the distribution ratio

$$\lim_{n\to\infty} \frac{1 - F(n)}{nf(n)} = \lim_{n\to\infty} \frac{m^{\theta} + n^{\theta}}{\theta n^{\theta}} \to \frac{1}{\theta} \tag{23}$$

---

confirms that the Champernowne distribution approaches asymptotically a form of Pareto distribution for large values of wages.

The second factor is the shape of individual preferences. First, we look at the utility function of the following CES form:

$$u = -\frac{1}{x} - \frac{1}{(1-l)}, \tag{24}$$

where the elasticity of substitution between consumption, denoted by x, and leisure, denoted by (1-*l*), δ = 0.5 (*l* is labour supply), has been used in numerical simulations. In the absence of taxation, the labour supply function is backward bending. From the careful analysis of the econometric evidence then available, Stern (1976) derives the central estimate of δ = 0.408. The relationship to the estimated coefficients is not straightforward, but some indication is given by the fact that a two standard error range in the substitution effect would lead by interpolating from Stern (1976, Table 2) to the interval for δ of around 0.2–0.6. The resulting difference in the optimum (linear) tax rate in the utilitarian case is between 36 per cent and 18 per cent (interpolating Stern, 1976, Table 3a).

The third factor is the SWF. A voluminous literature has explored how a range of specifications of the SWF, including those that capture a prioritarian objective, translate into quantitative optimal tax results. As in Mirrlees (1971), the SWF takes the form of:

$$W(u) = -\frac{1}{\beta}e^{-\beta u} \tag{25}$$

where β measures the degree of inequality aversion in the SWF of the government (in the case of $\beta = 0$, we define $W = u$).[26] If we write $W^{-\beta} = \int e^{-\beta u} f(n) dn$, then the limit as $\beta \rightarrow \infty$ is given by $W = \min_n[e^u]$. The curvature in the utility of consumption modifies marginal social welfare weights $W'U_x$ (MSWW) and makes the government preferences (implicit) more redistributive.[27] Mathematically, this MSWW is made up of two components: the increase in the individual's well-being due to an increase in consumption U_x and the increase in social welfare that arises from an increase in that individual's well-being W'. The distinction between the two components of an MSWW is important to understanding how prioritarianism differs from alternative

---

[26] Equation (27) is sometimes called the Kolm-Pollak SWF. It is invariant to a *translation* rescaling of utility, and indeed is the only prioritarian SWF with *this* invariance feature. If u(.) is a well-being measure, and u*(.) = u(.) + k, then a Kolm-Pollak SWF is such that the ranking of outcomes is the same using u(.) and u*(.). By contrast with the Atkinson SWFs, Kolm-Pollak SWFs do not require well-being numbers to be non-negative.

[27] See Kaplow (2010).

normative principles for optimal tax theory. In a prioritarian objective, the second component of the MSWW has a specific feature: the increase in social welfare due to an increase in an individual's well-being is decreasing in that individual's level of well-being. In formal terms, $\varphi(n) = \frac{W'U_x}{\lambda}$ decreases with n in a prioritarian objective even if U_x is constant because W' is decreasing in U and thus n. In words, the marginal value to society of an extra unit of consumption is greater if it goes to the worse off, even if individuals' utility from income is non-decreasing because a gain in utility for the worse off is worth more to society than a gain in utility for the better off. The implication of moving to a prioritarian objective from a utilitarian objective, and thus moving to a $\varphi(n)$ in expression (13) that declines more rapidly with n, is that marginal tax rates are greater along the income distribution, enabling greater redistribution to individuals earning less. This result is, of course, consistent with the intention to give priority to those with less well-being. To see more specific results on its optimal policy effects, however, we need to turn to numerical simulations.

The fourth factor is the government's revenue requirement specified as a fraction of total income not used for consumption by individuals, $R = 1\text{-}X/Z = 1 - \int x(n)f(n)dn / \int z(n)f(n)dn$. If $X/Z = 1$, then taxation is purely redistributive. R can be interpreted as the required revenue for essential public goods, and its size affects the cost of raising revenue to fund transfers to poor individuals, a key distributive tool in these models.

Before presenting the results, it may be useful to comment on some features of the simulation methodology, in particular in comparison to the method in Saez (2001). A key question is how the distribution of n is chosen. Ideally, we would like to use empirical earnings distributions in numerical simulations. This cannot apply directly, because the distribution of gross income z is affected by income taxation. This means that when we change utility function or its parameters, we also change the distribution of n so that the resulting distribution of z (absent the tax) remains the same. Otherwise, we get an effect through the changes in utility functions, but also through a change in the distribution of z. Inference of parameters from observed empirical earnings distributions is a long-standing issue in the optimal income taxation literature. In Saez (2001), the skill distribution is 'backed out' from the empirical distribution of income. To calculate the optimal tax schedule, Saez makes additional assumptions about the models structure. He calibrates the exogenous ability distribution such that actual T(.) yields empirical income distribution. He assumes that labour supply elasticity is constant (which implies a restricted form for the utility function). This assumption is contradicted by a growing body of evidence.[28] He further assumes a linear tax schedule in inferring the skill distribution from the earnings distribution. This is contradicted by tax schedules the world over, and seems particularly inappropriate in optimal nonlinear taxation. The strong assumptions required for structural identification of the model reduce the confidence of the optimal tax schedule calculations.[29] An alternative approach, one introduced in Kanbur and Tuomala (1994), is to accept the nonlinearities that characterise income tax schedules, and furthermore to allow for utility functions which imply non-constant labour elasticities. We cannot now back out the skill distribution as in Saez (2001). Rather, we should select a skill distribution, which, through the model, produces an earnings distribution that matches empirical earnings distributions. In other words, the income distribution inferred from the skill distribution matches the actual distribution. This is the method followed here.

The discussion of tax structures in optimal income tax literature has been almost entirely about marginal tax rates. As we mentioned in the introduction, average tax rates are arguably more important indicators of income tax progressivity. A high marginal tax rate as such performs no direct distributional function. Its purpose is to increase average tax rates higher up the income scale. In fact, in all cases shown in the tables and figures, average tax rates are increasing in income. It is difficult to establish this analytically, but computational techniques can demonstrate these patterns. The optimal tax structure in Figures 7–12 is depicted in terms of before-tax incomes.

Utilitarian and prioritarian SWFs and tax schedules:[30]   We give the following results in Figures 7–12 and Tables 6 and 7 by way of example of the orders of magnitude involved. First, the most direct effects of prioritarianism are apparent when we vary inequality aversion (i.e. through the parameter ß; where prioritarianism requires ß > 0). In Figures 7–10 and Tables 6 and 7, we show tax schedules for different levels of ß. (Note that in the tables and figures, these are marginal and average rates for all taxes that vary with income, and should be compared with the schedules for total of taxes on income and expenditures in real economies.) All the calculated tax schedules take the

---

[28] Using Norwegian data, Aaberge and Colombino (2006) provide support for declining elasticities. High labour supply elasticities among low-wage workers are also confirmed by empirical evaluations of various in-work benefit schemes operating in the United States, the United Kingdom and some other countries. By contrast, there is empirical evidence on the elasticity of taxable income that higher elasticities are among high-income individuals. See e.g. Gruber and Saez (2002).

[29] It is very appropriate in calculating top marginal rates.

[30] The results of the simulations are summarised in Appendix A.

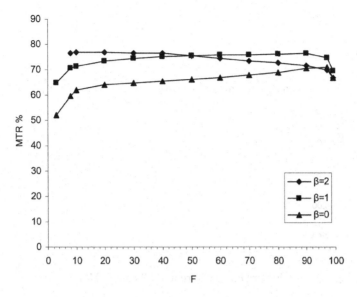

Figure 7a Marginal tax rates (MTR)

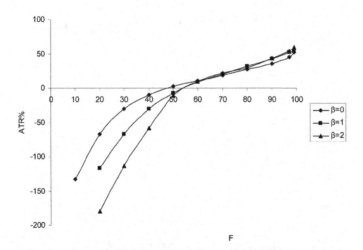

Figure 7b Average tax rates (ATR)

In both cases $\theta = 2.5$, $X/Y = 0.9$, utility function (24).

form of a lump sum credit (or basic income) followed by marginal tax rates. Our numerical results suggest that marginal tax rates tend to increase for all tax-payers with increasing inequality aversion. We might have expected that increasing β above 1 is likely to have a particularly large effect, but our calculations show that is not true. In fact, it can be seen that the difference in the marginal rates between the case $\beta = 1$ (or, when $\beta = 2$) and the maximin

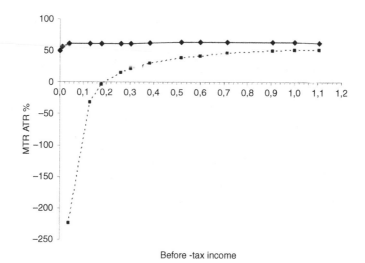

Figure 8a Utilitarian MTRs and ATRs

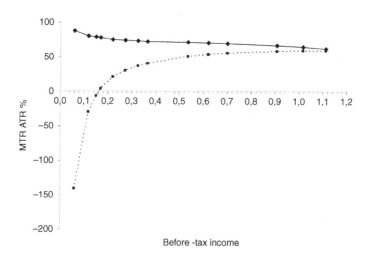

Figure 8b Maximin MTRs and ATRs

In both cases $\theta = 2.5$, $X/Z = 0.9$, utility function (24). Median $z = 0.18$ in 8a, Median $z = 0.15$ in 8b

solution ($\beta = \infty$) is not very large, whereas it is much more marked between the utilitarian case $\beta = 0$ and the case $\beta = 1$. Our results also seem to suggest that a sufficiently high level of inequality aversion leads to a pattern of optimally declining marginal tax rates, and indeed in the maximin case we find that marginal tax rates decline continuously with income. It may appear surprising that the maximin objective does not lead to increasing marginal tax rates, but

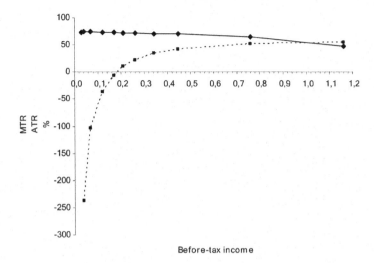

Figure 9a MTRs and ATRs, $\beta = 1$

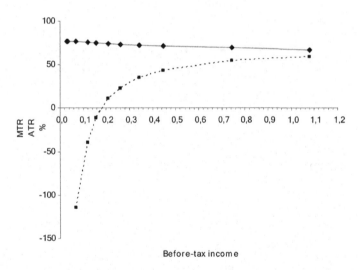

Figure 9b MTRs and ATRs, $\beta = 2$

In both cases $\theta = 2.5$, $X/Z = 0.9$, utility function (24). Median $z = 0.16$ in 9a, media $z = 0.16$ in 9b

this pattern follows from the fact that this objective is not concerned with inequality among those not in the 'least fortunate group'. On the other hand, average tax rates rise with income much steeper in the maximin case than in other cases considered in our simulations (see Figure 8b). The marginal tax rate curve crosses the average tax rate curve at the income level of $F(n) = 0.995$.

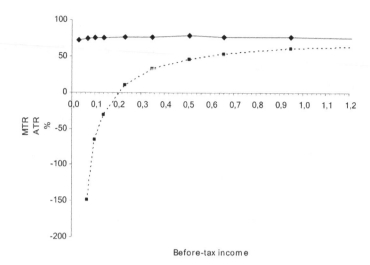

Figure 10a MTRs and ATRs, β = 1

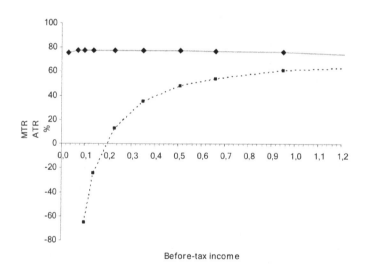

Figure 10b MTRs and ATRs, β = 2
In both cases θ = 2.0, X/Z = 0.9, utility function (24). Median z = 0.14 in 10a, Median z = 0.16 in 10b

Inherent inequality, redistributional preferences and tax schedule: To study how sensitive the shape of the tax schedule is to the choice of the parameter θ in the Champernowne distribution and redistributional preferences, we computed solutions when θ varies from 2.0 to 3.3 with CES utility function (24) and different β parameters. In other words, we gauged the sensitivity of the shape of

Table 6 Utility function (24), $\theta = 2.5$, X/Y = 0.9, F(n) = percentiles of wage distribution

F(θ)	β = 0.0 ATR%	β = 0.0 MTR%	β = 0.5 ATR%	β = 0.5 MTR%	β = 2.0 ATR%	β = 2.0 MTR%	β = ∞ ATR%	β = ∞ MTR%
0.10	−133.0	62.0	−198.0	70.0	−400.0	77.0		
0.50	3.0	61.0	−8.0	69.0	−12.0	75.0	−6.0	79.0
0.90	35.0	63.0	39.0	69.0	43.0	72.0	47.0	72.0
0.97	45.0	64.0	51.0	69.0	55.0	70.0	57.0	70.0
0.99	52.0	63.0	57.0	67.0	59.0	67.0	60.0	63.0

Table 7 Utility function (24), $\theta = 3.3, 2.0$, X/Y = 0.9, F(n) = percentiles of wage distribution

F(θ)	β = 0.0 θ = 3.3 ATR%	β = 0.0 θ = 3.3 MTR%	β = 1.0 θ = 3.3 ATR%	β = 1.0 θ = 3.3 MTR%	β = 0.0 θ = 2.0 ATR%	β = 0.0 θ = 2.0 MTR%	β = 1.0 θ = 2.0 ATR%	β = 1.0 θ = 2.0 MTR&
0.10	−50.0	58.0	−69.0	73.0	−275.0	62.0	−581.0	71.0
0.50	6.0	52.0	3.0	67.0	−18.0	66.0	−29.0	75.0
0.90	27.0	52.0	35.0	64.0	41.0	71.0	47.0	76.0
0.97	33.0	53.0	44.0	61.0	55.0	71.0	61.0	75.0
0.99	39.0	51.0	47.0	58.0	60.0	68.0	65.0	70.0

the tax schedule to the joint choice of the parameter θ in the Champernowne distribution and the parameter β, the degree of inequality aversion. Tables 6 and 7 show these cases. In Figure 8a, we see that with $\theta = 2.5$, the marginal tax rates increase for the lowest decile and then the marginal tax rates remain constant. In Table 7, we computed solutions when θ varies from 2.0 to 3.3 with CES utility function (24) and different β parameters. When $\theta = 3.3$, the marginal tax rates are declining. When $\theta = 2.0$ and $\beta = 0$, the marginal tax rate is increasing with income up to around the 98th percentile; when $\beta = 1$, it is increasing up to the 96th income percentile.

***Rank order social preferences*:** As an alternative SWF we calculate solutions for rank-order SWFs. Aaberge (2000)[31] provides a parametric variant for rank-order social preferences as follows.[32]

---

[31] See also Aaberge and Colombino (2006).
[32] These non-prioritarian SWFs satisfy the Pigou-Dalton condition.

$$W_q = \begin{cases} -\log F, q = 1 \\ \dfrac{q}{q-1}(1 - F^{q-1}), q = 2, 3, \ldots \end{cases}, \qquad (26)$$

where F denotes the percentile of the income distribution for an individual. When $q \to \infty$ W_q approaches the utilitarian case, then there is no concern of inequality. When q = 2, then $W_2 = 2(1 - F)$. This is in effect the weighting underlying the Gini coefficient, as shown by Sen (1974), who provided an axiomatic justification for such an SWF. In this case, the social marginal valuation declines linearly with F from twice the average for the lowest-paid taxpayer to zero for the highest-paid taxpayer. The optimal tax schedules with utilitarian and Gini weights differ considerably, with marginal rates being higher in the latter (see Figure 11). With Gini weights and the utility function in (27), marginal tax rates are increasing for the two lowest deciles.

The previous simulations (see e.g. Mirrlees, 1971; Atkinson, 1973; Tuomala, 1984; Kanbur and Tuomala, 1994) have used either the logarithmic utility of consumption or $U(x) = -1/x$. The important property of both of these functions is that the coefficient of relative risk aversion (the curvature of utility over consumption) is constant (= 1 and = 2 with fixed labour supply). In the light of table 1 in Chetty (2006), those values of the coefficient of relative risk aversion may be too high. Other preferences yield more complex relationships between net wage and labour supply. In the empirical labour supply studies, e.g. Keane and Moffitt (2001), preferences over working time and net income are given by the utility function that is quadratic in hours and net income. We also solve numerically cases in which utility function is quadratic in consumption (quadratic approximation) with a bliss point:

$$u = (x - 1) - a(x - 1)^2 - (1 - l)^{-1}, \quad x \in (0, 1) \qquad (27)$$

The utility of consumption in (27) is essentially less curvature than those used in the previous simulations. The coefficient of relative risk aversion in the utility function (27) in turn varies at different points of the function. With parameterisation used in our computations, the values of r are more in line with the empirical labour supply literature.[33] The striking thing in the numerical results shown in Figures 11a and 11b (see also Table 8) is that once we assume that preferences are given by the utility function that is quadratic in consumption, the shape of optimum tax schedules may be altered drastically. The marginal tax rates rise with income, practically speaking, over the whole range. The reason

---

[33] Using thirty-three sets of estimates of income and wage elasticities, the mean value of the coefficient of relative risk aversion calculated by Chetty (2006) is 0.71 in the additive utility case.

Table 8 Utility function (27), X/Y = 0.9

F(n)	β = 0.0 θ = 3.3 ATR%	β = 0.0 θ = 3.3 MTR%	β = 1.0 θ = 3.3 ATR%	β = 1.0 θ = 3.3 MTR%	β = 0.0 θ = 2.5 ATR%	β = 0.0 θ = 2.5 MTR%	β = 1.0 θ = 2.5 ATR%	β = 1.0 θ = 2.5 MTR%
0.10	−10.0	9.0	−83.0	25.0	−95.0	11.0	−403.0	25.0
0.50	5.0	14.0	1.0	33.0	−3.0	20.0	−14.0	39.0
0.90	14.0	26.0	23.0	44.0	19.0	39.0	30.0	54.0
0.97	20.0	36.0	33.0	49.0	30.0	50.0	41.0	59.0
0.99	25.0	41.0	37.0	50.0	37.0	54.0	48.0	59.0

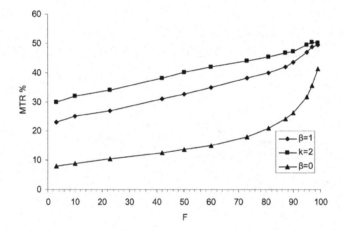

Figure 11a MTRs, θ = 3.3

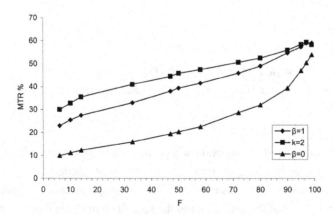

Figure 11b MTRs, θ = 2.5

In both cases X/Y = 0.9 utility function (27)

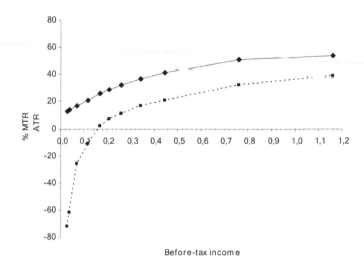

Figure 12a MTRs and ATRs, β = 0.0, θ = 2.5

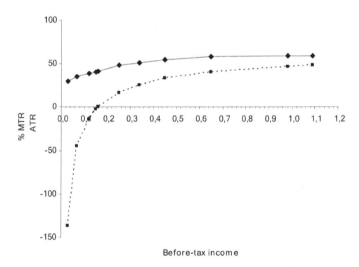

Figure 12b MTRs and ATRs, β = 1.0, θ = 2.5
In both cases X/Y = 0.9 and utility function (27). Median z = 0.15 in 12a, Median z = 0.12b

for this is that this utility function with upper bound on consumption implies necessarily a concave budget constraint in the Mirrlees model.

Next, we explore how sensitive is the level of lump sum transfer component (or basic income) of the tax system to the specification of the model. Tables 9 and 10 display the ratio of the basic income to the average net income with different redistributional preferences and when utility is either (24) or (27) and

Table 9 The ratio of x_o (basic income)[34] to the average
net income: utility function (24) and X/Y = 0.9

θ	β = 0.0	β = 1.0	Gini weights
3.3	0.52	0.66	0.62
2.5	0.61	0.69	0.67
2.0	0.62	0.70	0.65

Table 10 The ratio of x_o (basic income) to the average
net income: utility function (27), a = 5.0 and X/Y = 0.9

θ	β = 0	β = 1	Gini weights
3.3	0.06	0.25	0.33
2.5	0.15	0.35	0.42
2.0	0.25	0.44	0.51

Table 11 The extent of redistribution (RD); utility function (24),
P90/P50, X/Y = 0.9

θ	β = 0.0	β = 1.0	Maximin	Gini weights
3.3	22.6	34.0	36.8	33.0
2.5	37.3	47.5	50.7	44.3
2.0	47.0	60.0	61.7	60.5

revenue requirement is X/Y = 0.9. This ratio is clearly higher in the case of β = 1 and Gini weights 2(1-F) than in the case of the pure utilitarian β = 0. The ratio is increasing with pre-tax inequality. Since marginal tax rates may be a poor indication of the redistribution powers of an optimal tax structure, we measure the extent of redistribution, denoted by RD, as the proportional reduction between the percentile ratio (P90/P50) for market income, z, and the percentile ratio for disposable income, x.[35] Tables 11 and 12 show the extent of redistribution (in terms of our measure) in the case of utility functions (24), (27) and different distributional objectives. Is the pre-tax inequality (θ) more important than redistributional preferences (β) in determining the extent of redistribution? Perhaps the most interesting finding in our simulations can be seen in Table 11.

---

[34] x at the point n_0, denoted by x_0, and $l(n_0) = 0$.

[35] Unlike the scalar inequality measures, the use of fractile measures such as the percentile ratio allows us to consider changes in inequality at various points in the distribution.

Table 12 The extent of redistribution (RD): utility
function (27), a = 5.0, P90/P50. X/Z = 0.9

θ	β = 0.0	β = 1.0	Gini weights
3.3	8.0	24.1	28.2
2.5	26.0	35.5	44.4
2.0	39.0	54.0	57.3

It turns out that increasing β above 1 has a very modest effect on the extent of redistribution. This is true for all three values of θ. Hence, the extent of redistribution is about the same in the $\beta = 1$ case and in the maximin case.

It is also important to note that the extent of redistribution and the rising marginal tax rate may be two quite different things. The extent of redistribution is larger with higher β, but the marginal tax schedule may be rising in the case of $\beta = 0$ (see Figures 7a, 12a and 12b).

In sum, the optimal income tax schedule is very sensitive to a choice of the assumed form of utility of consumption. Unlike in most cases with the CES utility function (27) for the utility function quadratic in consumption, the marginal tax rate rises with income. Hence, the interaction between two components of an MSWW plays a central role in determining the shape of the tax schedule.

6 Optimal Separable Capital Income and Labour Income Taxation

One element left out of the foregoing theoretical analysis is capital income. We have seen a rising share of capital in many advanced countries since the 1980s (see Piketty and Zucman, 2014). This, in turn, directly increases inequality, because ownership of capital is much more unequally distributed than labour income. If we want to reverse the direction of past development in many advanced countries, we should look to an increased contribution from taxes on capital income. Should this mean a return to the system under which capital income is taxed at a higher rate than labour income? For example, until 1984, the United Kingdom had an investment income surcharge. What can we say about this question in the optimal tax framework?

There is much tax research implying that there is no need to impose any tax on capital or capital income. The often-cited result by Judd (1985) and Chamley (1986) that no capital taxation is optimal arises asymptotically in models with infinitely lived individuals. The significance of these findings is limited for a number of reasons. The Ramsey setting assumes both identical individuals and unavailability of an income tax. There is no redistribution problem and thus no need in principle to rely on distortionary taxation. Perhaps the most important doubts of the Chamley-Judd results come from Straub and Werning (2014). They show that, in both models, taxation may be positive even in the long run. They also argue that even when optimal taxes are zero in the long run, this may only be true after centuries of high taxation (see also Atkinson, 2014, p. 42).

Another result in the literature used in support of zero capital income taxation is the Atkinson and Stiglitz (1976) theorem interpreted in the intertemporal context. It says that under separable preferences, there should be no tax on capital income; it is more efficient to redistribute income by using solely a labour income tax. Atkinson and Stiglitz (1980, pp. 442–451) themselves were very well aware of the implausibly strong assumptions (most notably the absence of inheritance and the separability of preferences) behind their zero capital tax result. Atkinson (2014, p. 40) writes that: 'The result we stated is not a recommendation for zero capital taxation but delineation of a benchmark by which we can understand the conditions under which taxation is, or is not, desirable.' There is also an important difference between these two zero tax results. The Chamley-Judd results focus on given initial wealth whereas there is no inherited wealth in the Atkinson and Stiglitz result.

The Mirrlees model treats differences in observed income as due to unobserved differences in ability. Individuals do not differ only in ability, but also in initial endowments, denoted by ω. If we allow people to differ in their capital endowment, ω, with marginal density $f(\omega)$, generating capital income k (n, ω) and earnings $z(n, \omega)$, then we have to determine the tax schedule $T(z, k)$ in the face of the joint distribution $g(n, \omega)$. How to design $T(z, k)$? Can the optimum be attained with an income tax: $T(z + k)$? Can it be attained with a Nordic dual income tax: $T_z(z) + T_k(k)$? In other words, should we separate taxes on labour income and capital income (as in the Nordic dual income tax) or not?

Following Christiansen and Tuomala (2008), we employ a simple model where the economy lasts two periods. To introduce return to capital and the possible taxation thereof, it is useful to consider a two-period model wherein an individual starts out with the endowment ω. In Christiansen and Tuomala (2008), the initial endowment may be interpreted as representing various factors affecting capital income. It is also quite plausible to assume that in reality both ability and endowment are unobservable. This may be more plausible for intangible assets, but in practice there are a number of non-transparent ways in which even tangible assets can be transferred from one generation to the next.[36] First best taxation is not feasible in this economy, because we cannot distinguish ex ante between different types. There is asymmetric information in the sense that the tax authority is informed neither about individual skill levels and labour supply nor endowments.

Individuals are free to divide their first period (when young) endowment between consumption, denoted by c and savings, s. Each unit of savings yields a consumer $1+\rho$ additional units of consumption in the second period. Consumption in each period is given by

$$c(n) = \omega(n) - s(n), \tag{28}$$

$$x(n) = z(n) + (1+\rho)s(n) - T_l(z) - T_k(\rho s) \tag{29}$$

where $T_l(z)$ and $T_k(k)$ ($k = \rho s$) tax functions for labour and capital income.

Each individual supplies l units of labour in the second period. The labour market is perfectly competitive so that an individual's effective labour supply equals his or her gross income, $z = nl$. Labour is supplied (elastically) only in the second period and all taxes are imposed in that same period. The individuals have identical, separable, additive and quasi-linear consumption utility functions in the second period.

$$U = u(e - s) + x + (1+\rho)s + V(1 - l) \tag{30}$$

As in Christiansen and Tuomala (2008), wealth is in the individual's utility function.[37] The first-order conditions characterising the individual's choice of capital and labour income are:

$$\frac{V'(z/n)}{n} = 1 - t_z \quad \text{and} \quad u'(\omega - s) = 1 + \rho(1 - t_k) \tag{31}$$

where t_z and t_k are marginal tax rates on labour and capital income.

Following Saez (2001), we can derive an optimal tax formula by using a tax perturbation approach.[38] If one begins with some capital income tax schedule $T_k(k)$, assumed to be optimal, it must be that no slight adjustment

---

[36] This is a key point in Cremer, Pestieau and Rochet (2003).

[37] Saez and Stantcheva (2016) provide an excellent justification of wealth in the utility, both its technical role in this context and its history in economics and social sciences.

[38] Some earlier contributions use the tax perturbation method. Christiansen (1981) introduces the tax perturbation approach, but his main interest is the conditions under which the Samuelson rule is valid when nonlinear income tax and linear commodity taxes are available to finance the supply of public goods. Using a tax perturbation method, Piketty (1997) derives the optimal nonlinear income tax schedule under maximin without income effects. Roberts (2000) derives it also under the utilitarian case. A kind of perturbation is discussed in Diamond (1968). See also Gerritsen (2016).

to the schedule will change the level of social welfare. Furthermore, the linearization of the tax schedules leads to the absence of cross elasticities between savings and labour supply.[39] That is, an increase in t_k will leave savings unchanged and an increase in t_l will leave labour supply unchanged.[40]

The optimal nonlinear capital income tax can be expressed in the following way:[41]

$$\frac{t_k}{1 - t_k} = \frac{(1 - \varphi(k))}{\varepsilon} \frac{(1 - H(k))}{kh(k)}, \tag{32}$$

The marginal tax rate t_k is decreasing in the elasticity ε_k and the MSWW $\varphi(k)$, as expected. It is increasing in $(1 - H(k))$, the number of persons whose tax payments go up when the marginal tax rate on k rises, and decreasing in $h(k)$, which is the total output of those at income level k. Note, however, that (32) is derived under some restrictions, including quasi-linearity of preferences and a constant labour supply elasticity.

The revenue-maximising linear tax rate in the top bracket: We can also consider a constant top income tax rate above fixed k^* based on approximation or a linear tax above k^*. The elasticity of capital income ε_k is constant over the top income range (assuming individual utilities as in [30]), the change in capital income is $\varepsilon_k[k/(1 - t_k)]\Delta t_k$. The elasticity is defined positively as the proportionate change in k w.r.t. a proportionate change in $(1 - t_k)$ which accounts for the term $k/(1 - t_k)$. The total change in revenue is given by the sum over incomes k from k* upwards of $[(k - k^*) - t_k\varepsilon_k k/(1 - t_k)]\Delta t_k$. In the square bracket, only k varies so that we can replace this by its mean $\bar{k}$. The total change is now $[(\bar{k} - k^*) - t_k\varepsilon_k\bar{k}/(1 - t_k)]\Delta t_k$ and the revenue-maximising tax rate is then such that the square bracket is zero: $t_k/(1 - t_k) = (1 - k^*/\bar{k})/\varepsilon_k = 1/\alpha_k\varepsilon_k$ or $t_k = 1/(1 + \alpha_k\varepsilon_k)$, where α_k = Pareto parameter of the Pareto distribution. This follows from the fact that with the Pareto upper tail, the mean above k^* is $\alpha_k/(\alpha_k - 1)k^*$ so that $\alpha_k = \bar{k}/(\bar{k} - k^*)$. Intuition: higher α_k implies lower tax rates, and conversely. Such distributions have the key property that the ratio $\bar{k}/k^*$ is the same for all k^* in the top tail and equal to $\alpha/(\alpha - 1)$. k^* is the top x % threshold income and $\bar{k}$ is the average income of top x %.

---

[39] Hence both labour and capital income taxes satisfy the Mirrlees formula.

[40] Endowment effect: Making comparative statics from these first-order conditions $U_z = 1 - t_z(z) - V'(z/n) = 0$, $U_s = 1 - \rho(1 - t_k(\rho s)) - u'(\omega - s) = 0$ implies $\frac{dz}{d\omega} = 0$ and $\frac{ds}{d\omega} = U_{zz}^2 u'' U_{ss} > 0$.

[41] The optimal labour income tax can be derived by using the same procedure.

Table 13 Marginal capital income tax rates (%) with the
Champernowne distribution, $\epsilon = 1/3$

	$\psi(k) = 1/3$	$\varphi(k) = 1/3$	maximin	maximin
F(n)	$\theta = 2.0$	$\theta = 1.5$	$\theta = 2.0$	$\theta = 1.5$
0.10	89.2	93.1	94.7	95.2
0.50	66.5	73.0	81.2	89.0
0.90	52.5	59.3	70.4	68.4
0.99	48.5	53.3	67.0	63.0

Example: if $\varepsilon_k = 0.25$ (0.5) and $\alpha_k = 1.5$, $t_k = 72.7\%$ (57.1%).
Example: The optimal labour income tax above fixed z^* can be derived by
using the same procedure: if $\varepsilon_z = 0.25$ (0.5) and $\alpha_z = 3$, $t_z = 57.1\%$ (40%).

Given $\alpha_k = 1.5$ if the revenue-maximising top capital income tax rate t_k
would be equal to that observed (around 30 per cent) in Finland, the elasticity
ε_k should be 1.56. Note that until the 1970s, in many countries, the top tax rates
on capital income were often higher than the top tax rates on labour income.

The pattern of marginal capital income tax rates with quasi-linear
preferences: Assuming quasilinear preferences, constant elasticity, the
Champernowne-Fisk distribution (m,θ) and a prioritarian SWF, then the pattern
of marginal tax rates is given by:

$$\frac{t_k}{1 - t_k} = \left[\frac{1 - \varphi(k)}{\varepsilon_k} \right] \left[\frac{m^\theta + k^\theta}{\theta k^\theta} \right]. \tag{33}$$

Table 13 displays optimal marginal tax rates for different percentile points for
the Champernowne distribution.

Empirical facts on capital and labour income: A typical assumption earlier in
this Element and in the theoretical literature is that the tax authority can easily
differentiate taxes on labour income and on capital income, respectively. In
practice, however, this is far from easy, as has been realised and discussed at
length in connection with the dual income tax in the Nordic countries. Jäntti
et al. (2010) argue that the 1993 reform (the dual income tax system adopted) in
Finland had an impact on the level and composition of top incomes. There is a
great deal of evidence that wealthy taxpayers will shift income between the
labour and capital income tax bases to minimise their tax burden. There are a
number of papers analysing the elasticity of income shifting w.r.t. to tax

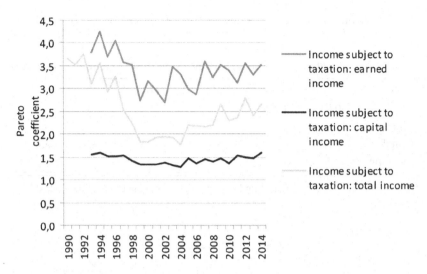

Figure 13 Pareto coefficients, α, in Finland 1990–2014.
Source: Riihelä et al., 2014

difference between labour and capital income in the Nordic countries.[42] Those papers generally find large income responses for owner-managers of closely held corporations. The owners who can afford to save can reduce their inter-temporal tax bill by taking less labour income out of the firm, which increases the net worth of the company. The increased net worth, in turn, increases the share of dividends that can be paid tax-free in the future. People who are not owners of closely held corporations do not have access to this route. Employees also generally do not respond to income-shifting incentives, as they usually do not have the possibility to do so.

In Figures 13–16, we present some facts about the distributions of labour and capital income in Finland and highlight their implications for optimal taxation. As in many other developed countries, in Finland, capital income is much more concentrated than labour income and net wealth, as shown in the Lorenz curves in Figure 14. At the top of the income distribution, total income comes mostly from capital income. At the top of 1 per cent, the share of capital income of total income varies between 50 per cent and 60 per cent and at the top 0.1 per cent makes up close to 80 per cent of total income. This fact implies that the Pareto parameter of the capital income distribution is not far from that of the total

---

[42] In Finland, Pirttilä and Selin (2011) and Harju and Matikka (2016) analyse the tax reforms of 1993 and 2005, respectively. In Sweden, Alstadsaeter and Jacob (2016) analyse the 2006 tax reform. There is also a strong evidence showing that the organisational form in dual income tax systems is strongly affected by the tax difference between corporate and non-corporate structures for small firms (Thoresen and Alstadsaeter, 2010)

Table 14		Correlations in 1987		Correlations in 2013		
	Net wealth	**Labour income**	**Capital income**	**Net wealth**	**Labour income**	**Capital income**
Net wealth	1.000			1.000		
Labour income	0.219	1.000		0.106	1.000	
Capital income	0.360	0.145	1.000	0.743	0.060	1.000

Data sources: Wealth Study Statistic Finland. Source: Riihelä et al. (2007, updated)

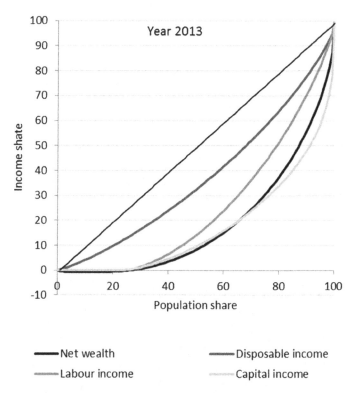

Figure 14 Lorenz curves in 2013 in Finland.

Source: Riihelä et al. (2007, updated)

income distribution. In fact, that was so in the beginning of the 2000s (see Figure 13).

Figure 15 documents a surge in capital incomes of top 1 per cent which starts just after the 1993 reform. Figures 15 and 16 show that top tax rates on upper-income earners have declined significantly after the 1993 reform. There is not

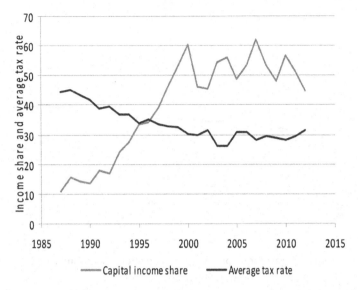

Figure 15 Capital income share and average tax rate for top 1 per cent in Finland 1967–2012.

Source: Riihelä et al. (2014)

much change in the composition of incomes among the next 4 per cent.[43] The gap between the tax rates on labour and capital incomes was huge after the 1993 reform.[44] The dual income tax dropped the marginal tax rates on capital income the more the higher was the person's total income before the reform. Those entrepreneurs who saw the largest reduction in the marginal tax rates on capital income also experienced the largest increase in capital income. At the same time, the share of labour income decreased for these taxpayers. The increase in the share of capital income out of total income was much more modest for high-income employees. It is obvious that in Table 14, the marked increase in the correlation between net wealth and capital income from 1987 to 2013 reflects income shifting.[45]

The often used argument against taxing the return to saving relies on the assumption that taxing saving creates inefficiencies and cannot help with redistribution. Other arguments against such taxation are related to the administrational considerations. One is that some of the most important assets are

---

[43] See Riihelä et al. (2014).

[44] 'The [Finnish] system seems to offer generous opportunities for tax-avoidance by transforming labour income into capital income. For example, retained corporate profits will increase the amount that is taxed as capital income, and capital gains on shares are only subject to capital income tax' (Lindhe et al., 2002).

[45] Tax on capital income in closely held companies is based on net wealth.

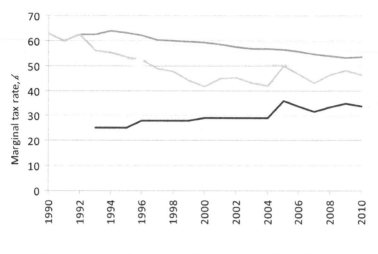

―――― Marginal tax rate for income subject to taxation (earned income)
―――― Marginal tax rate for capital income
―――― Marginal tax rate for income subject to taxation (earned and capital income)

Figure 16 Marginal tax rates.
Source: Riihelä et al. (2014)

likely to escape taxation, either because their returns are difficult to tax (imputed housing rents, personal businesses, human capital investment) or because there are reasons for preferential treatment (retirement saving). The other is the administrative complexity of taxing all forms of capital income, which was the one reason for the proportional rate adopted in the Nordic dual system. The main conclusion in Banks-Diamond (2010)[46] was that neither zero taxation, nor taxing total income, nor the Nordic dual income tax model were supported by the existing optimal capital income tax models.

Comprehensive income tax system $T(z + k)$: One of the lessons from the so-called Nordic dual income tax model is that the difficulty to distinguish in practice labour and capital incomes provides support for a so-called comprehensive income tax (i.e. taxing the sum of labour and capital incomes) – or, at least, for taxing capital and labour incomes at rates that are not too different. Hence, how the tax rate should be set if all income (whether stemming from capital or labour) were to be treated the same way for tax purposes. In many countries, most ordinary capital income, such as interest from a standard savings account, is taxed jointly with labour income by the individual income tax.

---

[46] See also Boadway (2012, pp. 85–104) and Bastani and Waldenström (2018).

Let H be the cumulative distribution of the total income distribution and h(y) the associated density (assuming again a linearized tax system at point y). Then, using the Saez (2001) procedure, the optimal nonlinear income tax on total or comprehensive income satisfies:

$$\frac{t_y}{1 - t_y} = \frac{(1 - \varphi(y))}{\varepsilon_y} \frac{(1 - H(y))}{yh(y)} \tag{34}$$

where $\varphi(y)$ is the average welfare weight on individuals with total income higher than y' and ε_y is the weighted average elasticity.

As noted by Saez and Stantcheva (2016), in this case the optimal tax formula turns out to take the same form as in Mirrlees (1971) and Saez (2001). It is also clear that the comprehensive income tax is the fully optimal tax if there is perfectly elastic income shifting between the labour and capital income bases when labour and capital are taxed differentially. Expression (34) is an example of a useable tax formula that can be combined with microeconometric research to produce definite conclusions for policy makers.

7 The Empirical Relationship between the Extent of Redistribution and the Components of the Mirrlees Framework

Next, we turn to examine empirically the relationship between the extent of redistribution and the components of the Mirrlees framework, with a focus on inherent inequality and governments' redistributive preferences. We have constructed our income distribution variables from the Luxembourg Income Study (LIS) database, which provides information on both factor and disposable incomes. Our data include fourteen advanced countries for approximately four decades.

The relationship that we study can be expressed as follows:

$$RD = \Phi(I, \varphi_{\{\varepsilon\}}, \underline{x}) \tag{35}$$

where RD is the extent of redistribution measured in terms of the relative reduction between factor-income and disposable-income inequality. We consider two summary measures, namely the Gini index and the percentile ratio P90/P50. Both measures are much used in inequality studies and provide somewhat complementary information. The Gini index is an overall measure of inequality, reflecting the behaviour of the whole income distribution, and being particularly sensitive to asymmetries in the central part of the distribution. Percentile ratios focus on two specific sections of the income distribution, providing an idea of how close (or distant) they are from each other. The P90/P50 ratio gives the ninetieth percentile relative to the median, focusing more on disparities at the top half of the distribution. Function Φ includes three components that reflect the ingredients of the Mirrlees model: I (factor-income inequality measure), φ (redistributional preferences) and ε (taxable elasticity). We do not have reliable estimates on ε, so we assume that the taxable income elasticity has not changed over the period considered. It is, however, implicitly in φ, because our redistributive preference measure is constructed using the optimal top tax formula (for given ε), for which we have collected data from various sources. In addition, $\underline{x}$ denotes control variables.

The LIS has harmonised microdata from (mostly) high- and middle-income countries, and the data are organised into different waves according to their date. The database provides information on both factor and disposable incomes.[47] In addition to the LIS historical data (Wave 0), we use the data from Wave I around 1980 to Wave IX around 2013.[48] In Appendix C, Table C1 illustrates – using Gini coefficients and P90/P50 ratios – that the inequality of factor incomes has risen in most countries over the sample period. In Figure 1, we presented the evolution of the extent of redistribution using the relative reduction in the Gini coefficient. Figure 17 depicts similar patterns using the P90/P50 ratios in measuring the extent of redistribution. In these two figures, the studied fourteen countries are categorised into three groups to provide a concise but readable illustration.[49] The figures show that the extent of redistribution has increased modestly in some countries. Thus, it appears that the redistributive role of government has corrected for some of the increase in inherent inequality.

We recognise that measuring governments' redistributive preferences is a challenging task. Indicators such as the optimal top tax rate might be endogenous (i.e. affected by both inequality and redistributive tastes of government). The so-called inverse-optimum research provides an alternative approach. A growing number of studies is trying to reveal social or distributional preferences behind tax/transfer policy. Those studies start from the existing tax-and-transfer system and reverse-engineer it to obtain the underlying social preferences. An explicit use of interpersonal comparisons to evaluate tax policy was introduced by Christiansen and Jansen (1978). They assumed that, over the period of time for

---

[47] Most studies on inequality and redistribution have utilised data sets including the largest possible number of countries all around the world (e.g. the panel data set of Deininger and Squire, 1996). However, such data sets have many problematic features, discussed in detail by Atkinson and Brandolini (2001).

[48] The lengths of different waves are not uniform. Moreover, some countries may have more than one observation within the same wave. For more information about the LIS waves, visit: www .lisdatacenter.org/our-data/lis-database/documentation/list-of-datasets/.

[49] The categorisation is the following: Anglo-Saxon (Australia, Canada, Ireland, the United Kingdom and the United States), Nordic (Denmark, Finland, Norway and Sweden) and Continental European (France, Germany, the Netherlands, Italy and Spain).

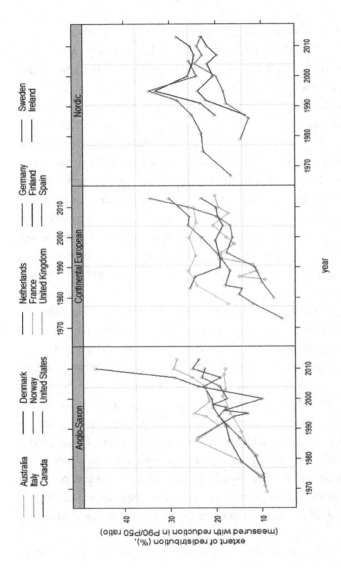

Figure 17 Evolution of the extent of redistribution, measured with the relative reduction in the P90/P50 ratio, in fourteen advanced countries (unbalanced data over the years 1967–2013). Authors' calculations from the LIS database

which they had data, the Norwegian government had been using the indirect tax system to maximise an additive symmetric SWF, which depends upon a single inequality-aversion parameter. They then estimated the model and solved the inverse-optimal tax problem. That is, what would the value of the inequality-aversion parameter have to have been, had their assumptions been correct? They found that the inequality-aversion parameter was quite far from the utilitarian value, thus confirming what many would have guessed, that Norway acts so as to give more social weight to low-income people. A similar study was carried out in India by Ahmad and Stern (1984); they found a similar outcome, namely that there was substantial inequality aversion.

Recently, detailed micro data on incomes and corresponding marginal tax rates have become available to study the social preferences implicit in tax-benefit systems. One of the first studies using micro data was by Bourguignon and Spadaro (2012). They consider the revealed social preferences of the French tax-benefit system. Jacobs, Jongen and Zoutman (2017) use this method to find the redistributive preferences of political parties implicit in the reform proposals combining the reform proposals with micro data on the income distribution and the elasticity of the tax base in the Netherlands. They find that all parties give a higher social weight to the poor than to the rich and that the differences between social welfare weights are rather small. Lockwood and Weinzierl (2016) apply the inverse-optimum approach over time to US tax policy and show that the implicit weights decline slowly with income, but the pattern is unconventionally flat. Bargain et al. (2014) estimate labour supply elasticities from micro data and characterise the redistributive preferences embodied in the welfare systems of seventeen EU countries and the United States under the assumption of optimality. They find that social welfare weights are always positive though not monotonically declining for low-income groups. They further find significant differences in social welfare weights over income between groups of countries (the United States vs. Continental/Nordic Europe vs. Southern Europe), with rather similar social welfare weights over income within groups of countries. Bastani and Lundberg (2017) use Swedish administrative data and provide a more detailed characterisation of income distribution, especially at the top. In addition, their data allow them to track changes over time for more than four decades.

From the optimal comprehensive tax formula (24) we obtain a redistributive preference measure, $\varphi = 1-\alpha\varepsilon t/(1-t)$, where we use data on top income tax rates (t), estimates for the Pareto coefficients (α) and values for taxable income elasticities (ε).[50] In our empirical application, we assume constant elasticities

---

[50] After calculating our estimates for φ, we only include positive values in our data set.

and present our results with a preferred estimate $\varepsilon = 0.20$. Figure 3 depicted the evolution of top tax rates in the fourteen countries of this study. Our main source for the top income tax rate data is Piketty, Saez and Stantcheva (2014), but we have updated the series using data from the OECD (2017) and the Association of Finnish Local and Regional Authorities (2017). The top income tax rates have decreased in all countries since the 1980s. We have constructed our data on Pareto parameters using top income shares from the World Inequality Database (formerly known as the World Wealth and Income Database, http://wid.world/, November 2017). We have observed an increase in top income shares in many countries since the 1980s (see for example Atkinson and Piketty, 2010), which is in line with the decrease in most countries' Pareto coefficients. The resulting variable, taste for redistribution measure (φ), does not have a common trend for all countries, but it has increased in most countries (see Figure C1 in Appendix C). Specifically, φ has increased in the Anglo-Saxon countries – reflecting that redistributive tastes of governments have decreased; the marginal consumption of high incomes has increased its value.

In addition, we have included other control variables that are presumably related to the extent of redistribution or the need for resources in the public sector. We use government employment share, dependency rate, unemployment rate, trade union density and openness measures for this purpose. For example, it has been argued that a larger government is 'needed' in more open economies. Rodrik (1998) gives an explanation that open economies are more subject to external shocks and that larger redistribution provides insurance and more stable income for individuals.[51] Our control variable data are primarily from the OECD. Table C2 in Appendix C provides more information about the data used in empirical investigations.

Empirical Specification and Results

We examine specifications of the following form (OLS models with dummy variables):

$$RD_{I;it} = d_0 + d_1 I_{factor;it} + d_2 \varphi_{it} + d_3 \text{ government employment}_{it}$$
$$+ d_4 \text{ dependency rate}_{it} + d_5 \text{ unemployment}_{it} + d_6 \text{ union density}_{it}$$
$$+ d_7 \text{ openness}_{it} + d_8 \text{ year}_{it} + \xi_i + \eta_{it}, \tag{36}$$

---

[51] In full assessment of the extent of redistribution, we should also take account of various services provided publicly at less than market value. These are considerable in the Nordic countries. Many of these items – health care, education and social services – are very extensive.

where i refers to a country and t to year, and d_0 is the constant term. The extent of redistribution (RD) is studied in relative terms; that is $RD_I = 100(I_{factor} - I_{disposable})/I_{factor}$, where I is either the Gini coefficient or the P90/P50 ratio. In addition to the taste for redistribution measure (φ), we include control variables and a linear term for time. Fixed country effects are denoted by ξ_i (traditional dummy variables), and the η_{it} are traditional error terms. The fixed country effects should take into account factors that stay constant over time within each country.

Table 15 presents models of type (36) with and without control variables. From models [1] and [2], where the dependent variable is RD_{Gini}, we learn that the Gini coefficient is positively related to the extent of redistribution, and our redistributive preference measure φ has a negative coefficient. These findings accord with the Mirrlees model. In models [3] and [4], where the dependent variable is $RD_{P90/P50}$, the factor-income inequality measure $P90/P50_{factor}$ is positively linked with the extent of redistribution and our taste for redistribution measure gets a negative coefficient – as one would expect based on the Mirrlees model.

We wish to note that some results in Table 15 with respect to our control variables are not robust to different specifications, although the main conclusions with respect to factor-income inequality and taste for redistribution hold in numerous specifications. For example, models [2] and [4] show a significant, negative coefficient for the dependency rate. However – as shown by Tanninen et al. (2018) – this negative association is not significant in more sophisticated specifications with flexible functional forms. In addition, we acknowledge that the interpretation of the public employment variable is complex: public employment can reflect governments' preference to redistribute, and it can be seen as a means to redistribute more effectively because high levels of public production may prevent some of the need to redistribute using taxes and transfers. For example, Pirttilä and Tuomala (2002, 2005) discuss the role of public production in an extension to the traditional Mirrlees model. A more detailed sensitivity analysis on the presented results can be found in Tanninen et al. (2018).[52]

---

[52] For example, Tanninen et al. (2018) study the robustness of chosen functional forms by using a flexible estimation method. In addition, the paper discusses results after changing the specification so that the same inequality indicator is not used on both sides of the estimation equation. Moreover, the paper checks the results when the extent of redistribution is measured in absolute terms (instead of relative terms). All these analyses provide results that are qualitatively in line with our main findings for I_{factor} and φ in Table 15. Tanninen et al. (2018) also investigate the main findings' robustness with respect to the chosen elasticity parameter. This was done by assuming alternative but 'reasonable' values for ε and using those when constructing the redistributive preference measure φ. With lower elasticity ($\varepsilon < 0.20$), the main results were qualitatively similar to those discussed earlier; with higher elasticity ($\varepsilon > 0.20$), the main results for φ were not statistically significant.

Table 15 Modelling the extent of redistribution: the coefficients (and standard errors) are provided; constant terms and country dummies are not reported. All models include observations from fourteen countries, and the number of observations is N = 105 in all models.

	Dependent variable: RD_{Gini}		Dependent variable: $RD_{P90/P50}$	
	[1]	**[2]**	**[3]**	**[4]**
$Gini_{factor}$	0.574***	0.530***		
	(0.132)	(0.167)		
$P90/P50_{factor}$			20.540***	21.608***
			(1.406)	(1.610)
φ	−6.818***	−4.949**	−5.277***	−4.204**
	(1.922)	(2.135)	(1.648)	(1.731)
government employment		0.228		0.320*
		(0.232)		(0.191)
dependency rate		−0.464**		−0.353**
		(0.203)		(0.167)
openness		0.039		0.039*
		(0.027)		(0.022)
unemployment		0.114		−0.109
		(0.124)		(0.096)
union density		0.006		0.047
		(0.100)		(0.083)
year	0.128**	0.068	0.134***	0.085*
	(0.051)	(0.064)	(0.040)	(0.047)
AIC	503.3	499.0	469.2	458.5

***, **, * denote significance at the 1, 5 and 10 per cent levels, respectively.

In summary, we have found support for the Mirrlees model: first, we find a positive relationship between the extent of redistribution (*RD*) and inherent inequality; second, we provide empirical evidence for the link between *RD* and governments' redistributive preferences. However, we are forced to acknowledge that our investigation suffers from shortcomings: measuring governments' taste for redistribution is hard to do well, and data availability is limited.

8 Other Considerations on Redistribution

8.1 Veblen Effect and Redistribution

Do people make comparisons between or among individuals of similar incomes? Or is the lifestyle of the upper middle class and the rich a more salient point of reference for people throughout the income distribution? As pointed out by Bowles and Park (2005), the Veblen effect has two special characteristics in which it differs from the usual consumption externalities. The Veblen effect is asymmetrical, because the individual reference group is the very rich or an intermediate group. The influence of the reference group may be substantially independent of its size.

If the Veblen effect is as important as a growing body of empirical studies seems to suggest, taxing consumption externalities might be welfare enhancing just in the same way as any other Pigouvian tax. This simple intuition does not tell us anything about the effects on the tax schedule. Does the Veblen effect lead a more progressive tax system or a less progressive tax system? Is income tax an effective tool for reducing inequalities and attenuating possible externalities arising from the Veblen effect? Some papers ask these questions in an optimal nonlinear tax framework;[53] see Oswald (1983), Tuomala (1990), Ireland (2001).[54] The two latter papers can say something on the shape of the tax schedule. Using numerical simulations, we study how the Veblen effect affects the extent of optimal redistribution.

Preferences are now represented by an additive utility function $u = U(x - v\mu) + V(1 - l)$, where x is a composite consumption good ($c = x - v\mu$ is effective consumption), μ is the consumption of the individual belonging to top one percentile, v refers to Veblen constant, and hours worked is l. To make computations easier, we assume μ and v are exogenous. Hence, our analysis differs from Oswald (1983) and Tuomala (1990), where μ, comparison consumption, is endogenous. A second difference is that the Veblen effect is asymmetrical while the usual consumption externalities are symmetrical. Otherwise the model is the same as the Mirrlees one.

As noted earlier, formulation of the SWF presents many difficult problems. For example, we must decide whether the government ought to accept the Veblen effect in social welfare. This is closely related to the awkward

---

[53] Aronsson and Johansson-Stenman (2008) address public goods provision in this framework.

[54] Boskin and Sheshinski (1978) and Blomquist (1993) consider linear income tax policy with relative consumption. Bowles and Park (2005) consider a simple two-class tax model. Their model takes each individual's reference consumption to be exogenous.

question of whether we should include antisocial preferences such as envy, malice etc. in SWF. If so, it would be important to consider the case where the government is 'non-welfarist' (paternalistic). It may be that people are willing to respect individual preferences based on a positive concern for the welfare of others, but they may not be prepared to accept negative interdependencies. But to the extent the Veblen effect is real, it should, of course, be respected when evaluating social welfare. We first assume that the government respects individual preferences, i.e. it is a 'welfarist' government. However, some elements in the Veblen effect may or may not be desirable from the social welfare point of view. Therefore, we also consider the case where the government is 'non-welfarist' (paternalistic) and its objective function may differ from that used by individuals. This approach is relatively common in conventional public economics, and has been used recently in the behavioural public economics literature as well.[55]

Note that when comparison consumption is exogenous, we get qualitatively the same results as in the standard nonlinear income tax model. Applying (13) Veblen effects enter through the terms A and C. Therefore, using numerical simulations, we can say more about the solution.

Again, we use a constant absolute utility-inequality aversion form for the SWF of the government (25). Simulations were carried out for the following utility function:

$$u = -\frac{1}{(x - v\mu)} - \frac{1}{(1 - l)}, \tag{37}$$

where μ is the consumption of the individual belonging to the top one per cent[56] and v refers to the Veblen constant. We assume again n to be distributed according to the Champernowne distribution.

In Figures 18a and 18b, we can compare optimum solutions without and with the Veblen effect. Marginal taxes are uniformly higher in the presence of the Veblen effect (with the same θ and mean). Figure 19b also shows that with higher pre-tax inequality ($\theta = 2$), we have here – practically speaking – a progressive marginal rate structure throughout. In the case of greater pre-tax inequality, low-income people are now poorer and require greater support, thus necessitating in turn higher marginal tax rates to meet the budget constraints. These higher marginal tax rates will of course have incentive

---

[55] Examples of the former include Kanbur, Keen and Tuomala (1994) and Pirttilä and Tuomala (2004), while O'Donoghue and Rabin (2003) and Bernheim and Rangel (2007) are examples of the latter. See Seade (1980) for seminal work.

[56] This corresponds to the consumption at the P99 point without the Veblen effect.

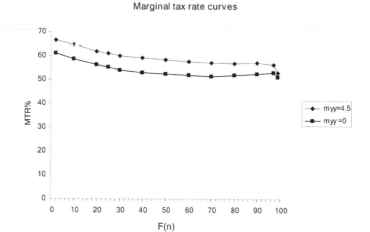

Figure 18a MTRs (X/Z = 0.9) U-function (28) θ = 3.3

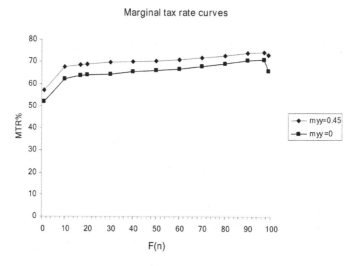

Figure 18b MTRs (X/Z = 0.9) U-function (28), θ = 2.0

effects, but this is traded off against the need for redistribution towards the very poorest. Labour hours are uniformly higher with the Veblen effect than without the Veblen effect with the same θ and mean (see Appendix A, Tables A1, A6, A24 – A30). With the CES utility function (37), we find that there is slightly more redistribution in the case with the Veblen effect (RD = 53.8%, θ = 2.0, β =0, Table 16) than in the case without that effect (47.0%, θ = 2.0, β = 0, Table 11).

Governments' and individuals' preferences differ: Non-welfarism vs welfarism:
It is not necessarily clear that a government ought to accept Veblen effects
when forming its social objectives. The utility function governing individuals' long-term welfare may be different from that of their short-term
welfare. Perhaps a stronger case for paternalism could be built on the idea
that the government is not willing to accept the consequences of the Veblen
effect. In other words, market behaviour is generated by one set of preferences, but the society evaluates it with respect to another set of preferences.
In many respects, the situation described earlier is fairly common in welfare
and normative public economics. Perhaps the most well-known example is
the analysis of so-called merit goods (Sandmo, 1983). The consumption of
these goods, in the viewpoint of the government, is meritorious and should be
encouraged or imposed, ignoring individual choice. Optimal taxation, when
the government attempts to alleviate poverty (e.g. Kanbur et al. 1994), is
another application of a much larger literature on 'non-welfarist' public
economics, where the social planner explicitly uses some other criterion for
evaluating an individual's welfare than the preferences of that individual.
Perhaps, at some level, one could also argue that redistribution – where the
government can evaluate individual welfare in a different way than the
individuals themselves – and correction of externalities are additional examples in which the SWF differs from the individual utility.

We assume now that the individual still maximises the same utility function
(37) as in the previous section, but the government's objective function rules out
the Veblen effect. Our numerical simulations show (Figures 19a and 19b) that
marginal tax rates are higher at the lower part of the distribution (below 30 per
cent) in the non-welfarist case than in the welfarist case, whereas it is other way
round at the top decile of income distribution.

The society may want to change individuals' choices on work hours. This
may happen indirectly, as in income taxation, or directly. The direct way would
be difficult to implement in practice. For example, in situations in which a rise in
income inequality will cause an increase in hours worked, individuals might
benefit if an outsider induced them to behave according to preferences they wish
they had.[57] In our numerical simulations, labour supply in turn is lower at the
lower part but larger at the upper part of distribution over the same range. Hours
worked are smaller in the non-welfarist case than in the welfarist case (Figures
20a and 20b).

Some other interesting results emerge from the comparison of these solutions. The value of n_0 is considerably higher in the non-welfarist case, with 3 per

---

[57] As our empirical results suggest in Tanninen and Tuomala (2008).

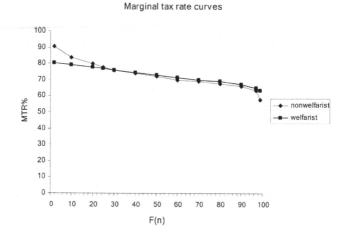

Figure 19a Marginal tax rates $\beta = 0.0$ X/Z $= 0.9$ $\theta = 3.3$

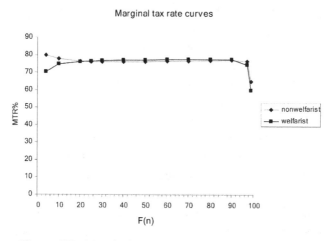

Figure 19b Marginal tax rates $\beta = 0.0$ X/Z $= 0.9$ $\theta = 2.0$

cent of the population choosing not to work.[58] In the welfarist case, almost everyone is brought into the labour force. We also find that there is just no differences in the extent of redistribution between the non-welfarist case and the welfarist case (see Table 16).

---

[58] $n_0 (> 0)$ is such an ability level that all individuals with $n \in (0, n_0)$ do not work, i.e. $l(n) > 0$, for $n > n_0$.

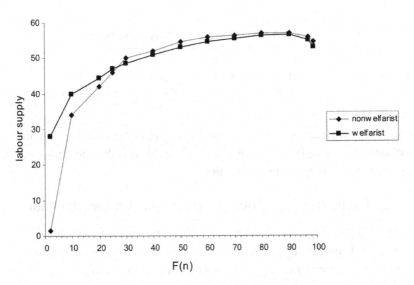

Figure 20a Labour supply, β = 1.0, X/Z = 0.9 θ = 3.3

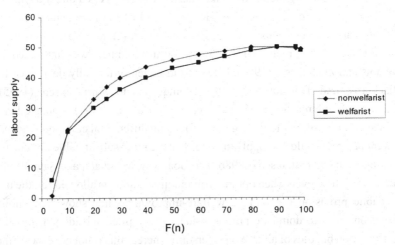

Figure 20b Labour supply β = 1, X/Z = 0.9, θ = 2.0

In sum: numerical results showed that the marginal tax rates and hours worked are higher at the optimum in the case of the Veblen effect than in the absence of the Veblen effect. The utilitarian (β = 0) optimal tax system is slightly more redistributive with the Veblen effect than in the absence of it.

Table 16 The extent of redistribution (RD); utility function (28), X/Y = 0.9.

θ	$\beta = 0.0$	$\beta = 1.0$	Non-welfarism $\beta = 1.0$
3.3	29.2	33.3	33.2
2.0	53.8	59.2	60.0

Our results provide support for the view that optimal tax policy may mitigate externalities arising from the Veblen effect. We also find that the Veblen effect rises the extent of optimal redistribution.

8.2 Public Provision, Public Employment and Redistribution

Standard optimal tax models simplify reality in many ways to focus on specific questions. Unfortunately, in many cases these simplifications may affect the results. For example, the interplay between marginal rates and public provision is missing in the standard optimal income tax model. Blomquist, Christiansen and Micheletto (2010) examine the implications of public provision for tax distortions. They suppose public provision is strictly tied to working hours (e.g. day care) and paid by the income tax. Then part of the tax is a direct payment, like a service fee or market price. Hence, not all of the marginal tax rate is distortionary, and one must also look at how tax revenue is spent as well as raised to get the full picture. The intuition of this argument was first noted by Nichols and Zeckhauser (1982), but was subsequently formally developed by Blackorby and Donaldson (1988), Blomquist and Christiansen (1995), Boadway and Marchand (1995) and Cremer and Gahvari (1997), among others. Note that this is similar to the argument for using differential commodity taxes: lower tax rates should also apply to goods that are more substitutable for leisure. Blomquist and Christiansen (1998b) and Boadway, Marchand and Sato (1998) have shown that, even when optimal commodity taxation is allowed for, the use of public provision can still be welfare-improving. They show that public provision tends to dominate price subsidies, since price subsidies distort the consumption bundles of all true type persons, whereas this is not necessarily the case for public provision.

Pirttilä and Tuomala (2005) analyse the potential role of public sector employment and public investment as redistributional devices along with a nonlinear income tax. When discussing public sector employment, it is also natural to examine the use of public capital in connection to public production. As shown in several empirical studies, the accumulated stock of public capital is an important factor in enhancing the productivity capacity of the economy.

Thus, decisions on public investment taken by the government today have long-lasting effects on the well-being of both present and future generations. Therefore, the choice of discount rate that ought to be used in evaluating public projects is one of the most important decisions taken by the government. It is not only important for accepting or rejecting a specific project but, in particular, for the allocation of resources between the public and the private sectors of the economy. A key assumption of their approach is that the wage rates of different types of workers depend on their relative supplies and complementarity with capital. Another key assumption is that there are two production sectors in the economy (private and public) which both use low-skilled and skilled labour, but the factor intensities and complementarity with capital may differ. Using a two-type and two-sector optimal nonlinear income tax model with endogenous wages, they analyse the decision rules governing public employment policy, capital allocation between the private and public sectors, and the size of the public sector in a two-type and two-sector optimal nonlinear income tax model with endogenous wages. The government can reduce wage inequality in the private sector by employing more unskilled workers and fewer skilled workers than is necessary to minimise cost at the prevailing gross wage rate and, if skilled labour and capital are complementary, by favouring public sector capital accumulation. Therefore, production efficiency holds neither in public employment decision nor in capital allocation. The effects of public employment and investment on income inequality increase when the size of the public sector increases. The optimal size of the public sector is also shown to be relatively large when public employment and investments reduce wage inequality. These results help to explain the growth in the public-sector size and why a larger government does not necessarily hamper growth.

8.3 Endogenous Wages in the OLG Model and Redistribution

Several earlier papers have analysed the intertemporal dimension of direct taxation in the overlapping generations (OLG) model. An early contribution is by Ordover and Phelps (1979).[59] Stiglitz (1987) extends the analysis to include general equilibrium considerations arising from endogenously determined pre-tax wage rates. Brett (1997), using the self-selection interpretation of optimal taxation, describes capital income taxation rules if preferences are not separable. In an OLG model, Boadway, Marchand and Pestieau (1998) treat labour and capital income taxation separately, in the spirit of the so-called dual income tax system. In their model bequests have a key role. Atkinson and

---

[59] The authors also did some earlier work; see the references cited in Ordover and Phelps (1979).

Sandmo (1980) examine optimal savings income taxation under the case where there is no heterogeneity within generations.[60]

Pirttilä and Tuomala (2001) combine two well-known economic models: the Mirrlees (1971) model of optimal taxation and the overlapping generations model as represented in Diamond (1965). The reason for this is that this combination, encompassing heterogeneity both within and between generations, provides an appropriate means to study savings taxation and public goods provision in a dynamic model with distortionary taxation. They allow for a rich description of the production technology that enables the before-tax wage rate to depend on e.g. the labour supply of different individuals. This is a quite plausible and important assumption in an essentially long-term, dynamic framework.

In a general equilibrium setting in which wages are not given, capital taxes or subsidies may be optimal if they favourably influence the distribution of pre-tax income through the effects of changes in the capital stock on wage rates. In this instance and more broadly, when the government cannot directly control the capital stock through debt or other policies, taxation or subsidisation of capital serves as a substitute instrument. Allowing for endogenously determined wages is also important because it gives rise to new forms of distortionary taxation and production inefficiency, along the lines of Naito (1999).

In sum: taxation and public provision can affect the pre-tax or the market distribution of income. Hence, we cannot rely only on fiscal redistribution in dealing with the symptoms of underlying income inequality. In other words, mechanisms of fiscal redistribution may not be sufficient, but will have to be supplement by forms of pre-distributive tools such as public provision and public production.

8.4 Income Uncertainty and Redistribution

The Mirrlees (1971) model treats differences in observed income as being due to unobserved differences in ability, which means that individuals know exactly what income they will receive at each possible level of effort. We know that this is not always the case. One might well argue that people do not owe their (un) success entirely to ability, but part of the income differentials are due to luck. The critical question is whether differences in income come mostly from luck or from ability. There is another strand of optimal redistribution literature (see Mirrlees, 1974; Varian, 1980; Tuomala, 1984; Low and Maldoom, 2004; Pirttilä

---

[60] Using the same approach, Park (1991) relaxes the homogeneity assumption but does not derive many concrete results.

and Tuomala, 2007; Kanbur, Pirttilä and Tuomala, 2008; Boadway and Sato, 2011) stressing the social insurance role of redistributive taxation. In this moral hazard (hidden action) framework, an increase in variability of income would also increase the optimal degree of progressivity, because it increases the insurance value of progressive taxation. In other words, if the role of luck is significant in determining income, it is reasonable to have progressive taxation – it is a form of social insurance in which the lucky subsidise the unlucky. In this setting income is partly due to individual effort and partly due to luck, but the government can only observe realised income, not effort.[61] The optimal redistribution scheme is a balance between providing the workers with adequate incentives to acquire skills and sufficient insurance. Low and Maldoom (2004) show how the degree of progressivity reflects a trade-off between an insurance effect, which favours progressivity in the sense of increasing marginal tax rates, and an incentive effect, which works against such progressivity. As shown in Tuomala (1984), we cannot say analytically on the progressivity in the sense of an increasing marginal tax rates with income. Note, however, that in this setting it is not possible to prove the zero marginal tax rate at the top. In fact, it is more likely the marginal tax rate of top incomes is rather high. While the probability of being the most productive in society is so small, the incentive losses from the severe taxing of the ex post most productive taxpayer is in turn very small. By and large, the tax schedule in this simple model is so complicated that it is difficult to say much about the shape of the optimal tax schedule without numerical solutions for some specific examples.

Scholars have devoted little attention to studying optimal income taxation when both ability differences and earnings uncertainty are present. Hence, we have the standard moral hazard cum adverse selection model. Eaton and Rosen (1980) considered the choice of a linear progressive income tax in a model with two ability types and uncertain earnings. Given the difficulty of obtaining analytical results in even this simple setting, they solved some numerical examples. Depending on the parameters chosen, such as the degree of risk aversion, adding uncertainty to the standard optimal redistribution problem with two ability-types could either increase or decrease the optimal linear tax rate. Tuomala (1978, 1990) considers in the nonlinear taxation when individuals do not fully know their productivity skills in

---

[61] Mirrlees (1990) and Hsu and Yang (2013) analyse linear income tax with uncertainty. Both papers show that adding uncertainty always increases the marginal tax rate of the linear income tax.

making labour supply decisions. Again, given the complexity of the problem, numerical solutions are needed. It seems to us that the right kind of model in which to examine the question of implications of luck and ability is one in which some labour decisions are made early, under imperfect information, while others are made at the last moment, under full information. Along these lines, Tuomala (1986) considers a model in which individuals first decide how much educational training to have without accurately knowing their own abilities. Educational training reveals their abilities to themselves, and on the basis of known abilities they make their labour supply decisions.

9 Conclusions

We employed the standard Mirrlees model and its extensions to address the issue of how the optimal income redistribution changes when the different factors of the model change. We focused our attention both on the top tax rate and on the entire tax schedule. Numerical results in Kanbur and Tuomala (1994) and Tuomala (2016) show, and our new numerical results strengthen the case, that the optimal income tax/transfer system becomes more progressive when pre-tax income inequality increases, taxing the better off at higher rates to support the less well off. Thus, one of the policy responses in view of increasing pre-tax income inequality should be a greater willingness to redistribute through the tax-and-transfer system. Correspondingly, if inherent inequality decreases, governmental redistribution decreases. Our results suggest that the shift in tax burden from the top to further down in the distribution which we have seen over the past few decades in many advanced countries cannot be justified in the standard optimal tax model, which embodies conventional assumptions about inequality aversion and the trade-off between equity and efficiency. In utilitarian, prioritarian (giving priority to worse-off individuals) and maximin cases, an appropriate response to rising inequality is a shift towards a more progressive income tax system.

A rising capital share has increased income inequality in many developed countries. This can be countered by fiscal or other means. Equity considerations suggest capital income should be taxed more than labour income. The often used argument against taxing the return to saving relies on the assumption that taxing saving creates inefficiencies and cannot help with redistribution. These considerations in turn suggest going in a different direction. Other arguments against such taxation are related to administrational considerations such as that some of the most important assets are likely to escape taxation, either because their returns are difficult to tax or because there are reasons for preferential treatment (retirement saving). The administrative complexity of taxing all forms of capital income was the one reason for the proportional rate adopted in the Nordic dual system. Often many of these reasons against taxing capital or capital income are political excuses to do nothing to minimise tax avoidance. It is clear that international cooperation in fiscal matters makes it easier to implement taxes on capital.

A growing empirical literature analyses how differences in capital and labour income taxation affect income shifting. The general result from this literature is that income shifting responds strongly to tax incentives along both the intensive (shifts between tax bases) and extensive margins (organisational shifts). This implies that both behavioural margins are important when determining the effects of taxes on income shifting. Along the intensive margin, these effects are heterogeneous because owner-managers of firms have much easier access to income shifting than employees. Along the extensive margin, the effects seem to be stronger for small firms as the organisational form for large firms is mostly determined by non-tax factors.

Given these considerations, how should capital income be taxed? Roughly classifying we can distinguish four alternatives to tax capital income: not at all, linearly (Nordic dual income tax), relating the marginal tax rates of capital and labour incomes and taxing all income on the same schedule. Hence, the difficulty to distinguish in practice labour and capital incomes provides support for a so-called comprehensive income tax (i.e. taxing the sum of labour and capital incomes) – or, at least, for taxing capital and labour incomes at rates that are not too different.

So large has been the increase in the share of income going to the top 1 per cent that taxing them more heavily would only return them to the level of total income they had some decades ago. In fact, one of the reasons that top earners have done so well is rent-seeking. Taxing rent would not only reduce inequality but also reduce incentive for rent-seeking activities.

We examined empirically the relationship between the extent of redistribution and the components of the Mirrlees model using inequality measures (Gini coefficient and percentile ratio P90/P50) calculated from the LIS database. We also made an attempt to measure governments' taste for redistribution; we did this by collecting data from various sources and utilising the optimal top tax formula. We found a positive link between inherent (factor-income) inequality and the extent of redistribution, and we found an association between our redistributive preference measure and the extent of redistribution. Our findings support the Mirrlees model.

Finally, we should note that reductions in income inequality were achieved in the past not only via fiscal redistribution but also by reducing inequality in market income. In other words, mechanisms of fiscal redistribution may not be sufficient, but will have to be supplemented by forms of pre-distributive tools such as investment in education and skills and public production. In addition, the determination of earnings is not simply a matter of market forces, and important roles are played by the social norms which influence the behaviour of employers and workers.

Appendix A

The results of the simulations are summarised in Tables A1–A30. The tables give labour supply, l, gross income, z, net income, x, and optimal average (ATR), marginal tax rates (MTR), E^u (uncompensated elasticity) and I (income effects) at various percentiles of the ability distribution (F(n) = cumulative distribution function). X/Z = 0.9 or 1-X/Z = 0.1 (R = revenue requirement) in all cases. The tables also provide the percentile ratio (P90/P10) and (P90/P50) for net and gross incomes. We measure the extent of redistribution, denoted by RD, as the proportional reduction between the percentile ratio for market income, z, and the percentile ratio for disposable income, x.

Table A1 $u = -\frac{1}{x} - \frac{1}{(1-l)}$

$\beta = 0.0$	$\theta = 3.3$	X/Z = 0.9					
F(n)	l	Z	x	ATR%	MTR%	E^u	I
0.10	0.50	0.09	0.14	−50.0	58.0	0.18	−0.22
0.50	0.55	0.20	0.19	6.0	52.0	−0.003	−0.30
0.90	0.53	0.38	0.28	27.0	52.0	−0.09	−0.37
0.97	0.51	0.54	0.35	33.0	53.0	−0.13	−0.41
0.99	0.49	0.72	0.44	39.0	51.0	−0.18	−0.46
P90/P10		4.22	2.0				
RD(%)			52.6				
P90/P50		1.9	1.47				
RD(%)			22.6				
$n_0 = 0.02$	$x_0 = 0.1$	$F_0 = 0.0$					

Table A2 $u = -\frac{1}{x} - \frac{1}{(1-l)}$

$\beta = 1.0$	$\theta = 3.3$	X/Z = 0.9					
F(n)	l	Z	x	ATR%	MTR%	E^u	I
0.10	0.36	0.07	0.14	−100.0	73.0	0.53	−0.18
0.50	0.49	0.18	0.18	3.0	67.0	0.13	−0.26
0.90	0.53	0.38	0.25	35.0	63.0	−0.04	−0.34
0.97	0.52	0.56	0.33	44.0	61.0	−0.11	−0.40
0.99	0.50	0.75	0.39	47.0	58.0	−0.17	−0.44

Table A2 (cont.)

$\beta = 1.0$	$\theta = 3.3$	X/Z = 0.9	
P90/P10		4.22	2.0
RD(%)			52.6
P90/P50		2.11	1.39
RD(%)			34.0
$n_0 = 0.05$	$x_0 = 0.12$	$F_0 = 0.0$	

Table A3 $u = -\frac{1}{x} - \frac{1}{(1-l)}$

$\beta = 0.0$	$\theta = 2.5$	X/Z = 0.9					
F(n)	l	z	x	ATR%	MTR%	E^u	I
0.10	0.41	0.06	0.14	−133.0	62.0	0.38	−0.19
0.50	0.50	0.18	0.19	3.0	61.0	0.08	−0.28
0.90	0.50	0.44	0.29	35.0	63.0	−0.04	−0.36
0.97	0.47	0.73	0.39	45.0	64.0	−0.1	−0.43
0.99	0.45	1.05	0.50	52.0	64.0	−0.16	−0.48
P90/P10		7.33	2.07				
RD/%)			71.8				
P90/P50		2.44	1.53				
RD(%)			37.3				
$F_0 = 0.0$	$x_0 = 0.12$	$n_0 = 0.03$					

Table A4 $u = -\frac{1}{x} - \frac{1}{(1-l)}$

$\beta = 1.0$	$\theta = 2.5$	X/Z = 0.9					
F(n)	L	z	x	ATR%	MTR%	E^u	I
0.10	0.28	0.04	0.14	−200.0	74.0	0.92	−0.17
0.50	0.45	0.16	0.18	−7.0	73.0	0.23	−0.24
0.90	0.50	0.45	0.26	42.0	69.0	−0.02	−0.34
0.97	0.51	0.76	0.36	52.0	64.0	−0.14	−0.34
0.99	0.53	1.16	0.53	54.0	56.0	−0.30	−0.52
P90/P10		11.3	1.9				
RD(%)			6.1				
P90/P50		2.7	1.42				
RD(%)			47.5				
$F(n_0) = 0.0$	$x_0 = 0.13$	$n_0 = 0.05$					

Table A5 $u = -\frac{1}{x} - \frac{1}{(1-l)}$

β = 2	θ = 2.5	X/Z = 0.9					
F(n)	l	Z	x	ATR%	MTR%	E^u	I
0.10	0.22	0.03	0.15	−400.0	77.0	0.92	−0.17
0.50	0.42	0.16	0.17	−12.0	75.0	0.23	−0.24
0.90	0.50	0.46	0.25	43.0	72.0	−0.02	−0.34
0.97	0.495	0.75	0.34	55.0	70.0	−0.14	−0.34
0.99	0.48	1.08	0.44	59.0	67.0	−0.30	−0.52
P90/P10		14.7	1.7				
RD(%)			88.4				
P90/P50		2.83	1.47				
RD(%)			48.1				
$F_0 = 0.01$	$n_0 = 0.066$		$x_0 = 0.14$				

Table A6 $u = -\frac{1}{x} - \frac{1}{(1-l)}$

β = 0	θ = 2	X/Z = 0.9					
F(n)	l	Z	x	ATR%	MTR%	E^u	I
0.10	0.30	0.04	0.15	−100.0	62.0	0.82	−0.17
0.50	0.45	0.17	0.19	−18.0	66.0	0.19	−0.26
0.90	0.47	0.51	0.30	41.0	71.0	0.002	−0.36
0.97	0.45	0.95	0.43	55.0	71.0	−0.1	−0.44
0.99	0.44	1.58	0.63	60.0	68.0	−0.22	−0.53
P90/P10		12.7	2.0				
RD(%)			84.3				
P90/P50		3.0	1.58				
RD(%)			47.0				
$n_0 = 0.02$	$x_0 = 0.13$	$F_0 = 0.0$					

Table A7 $u = -\frac{1}{x} - \frac{1}{(1-l)}$

β = 1	θ = 2	X/Z = 0.9					
F(n)	l	Z	x	ATR%	MTR%	E^u	I
0.10	0.177	0.02	0.15	−100.0	71.0	1.8	−0.16
0.50	0.38	0.14	0.19	−31.0	75.0	0.38	−0.23
0.90	0.46	0.50	0.27	46.0	77.0	0.05	−0.34
0.97	0.46	0.95	0.376	60.0	76.0	−0.07	−0.41
0.99	0.45	1.55	0.52	66.0	75.0	−0.22	−0.48

Table A7 (cont.)

$\beta = 1$	$\theta = 2$	$X/Z = 0.9$	
P90/P10		25.0	1.74
RD(%)			93.0
P90/P50		3.57	1.42
RD(%)			60.0
$n_0 = 0.0685$	$x_0 = 0.148$	$F_0 = 0.03$	

Table A8 $u = -\frac{1}{x} - \frac{1}{(1-l)}$

$\beta = 2.0$	$\theta = 2$	$X/Z = 0.9$					
F(n)	l	Z	x	ATR%	MTR%	E^u	I
0.10	0.13	0.02	0.15	−843.0	74.0	2.62	−0.15
0.50	0.37	0.13	0.18	−34.0	78.0	0.45	−0.22
0.90	0.47	0.51	0.27	48.0	77.0	0.025	−0.047
0.97	0.47	0.98	0.37	62.0	76.0	−0.086	−0.41
0.99	0.47	1.59	0.53	66.0	71.0	−0.212	−0.50
P90/P10		31.9	1.72				
RD(%)			94.6				
P90/P50		3.9	1.5				
RD(%)			61.5				
$n_0 = 0.073$	$x_0 = 0.149$	$F_0 = 0.038$					

Table A9 Maximin $u = -\frac{1}{x} - \frac{1}{(1-l)}$

Maximin	$\theta = 3.3$	$X/Z = 0.9$					
F(n)	l	Z	x	ATR%	MTR%	E^u	I
0.11	0.10	0.02	0.13		88.0	3.66	−0.13
0.50	0.47	0.17	0.16	5.0	74.0	0.20	−0.24
0.90	0.54	0.39	0.23	40.0	65.0	−0.05	−0.33
0.97	0.54	0.56	0.30	47.0	61.0	−0.12	−0.39
0.99	0.53	0.74	0.37	50.0	56.0	−0.19	−0.44
P90/P50		2.23	1.41				
RD(%)			36.8				
$n_0 = 0.17$	$x_0 = 0.13$	$F_0 = 0.07$					

Table A10 $u = -\frac{1}{x} - \frac{1}{(1-l)}$

Maximin	$\theta = 2.5$	X/Z = 0.9					
F(n)	l	Z	x	ATR%	MTR%	E^u	I
0.11	0.005	0.001	0.14		88.0		−0.12
0.50	0.42	0.15	0.16	−6.0	79.0	0.33	−0.22
0.90	0.52	0.45	0.23	47.0	72.0	−0.01	−0.33
0.97	0.51	0.74	0.32	57.0	70.0	−0.11	−0.40
0.99	0.51	1.08	0.43	60.0	63.0	−0.21	−0.47
P90/P50		2.96	1.46				
RD(%)			50.7				
$n_0 = 0.16$	$x_0 = 0.14$	$F_0 = 0.11$					

Table A11 $u = -\frac{1}{x} - \frac{1}{(1-l)}$

Maximin	$\theta = 2.0$	X/Z = 0.9					
F(n)	l	z	x	ATR%	MTR%	E^u	I
0.17	0.003	0.0006	0.15		86.0		
0.50	0.34	0.13	0.17	−37.0	81.0	0.55	−0.21
0.90	0.48	0.52	0.26	51.0	78.0	0.04	−0.33
0.97	0.48	0.97	0.36	63.0	76.0	−0.09	−0.41
0.99	0.47	1.55	0.51	67.0	71.0	−0.21	−0.49
P90/P50		4.0	1.53				
RD(%)			61.7				

Table A12 $u = -\frac{1}{x} - \frac{1}{(1-l)}$

	$\theta = 3.3$	X/Z = 0.9					
F(n)	l	Z	x	ATR%	MTR%	E^u	I
0.10	0.41	0.08	0.14	−85.0	68.0	0.38	−0.20
0.50	0.50	0.18	0.18	2.0	66.0	0.11	−0.26
0.90	0.52	0.37	0.25	34.0	62.0	−0.04	−0.34
0.97	0.51	0.55	0.32	43.0	60.0	−0.11	−0.40
0.99	0.50	0.74	0.40	39.0	57.0	−0.17	−0.44
P90/P10		4.62	1.78				
RD(%)			61.6				
P90/P50		2.06	1.38				
RD(%)			33.0				
$n_0 = 0.04$	$x_0 = 0.12$	$F_0 = 0.0$					

Table A13 Rank Order $u = -\frac{1}{x} - \frac{1}{(1-l)}$

	$\theta = 2.5$		X/Z = 0.9				
F(n)	l	z	x	ATR%	MTR%	E^u	I
0.10	0.31	0.05	0.15	−200.0	71.0	0.7	−0.17
0.50	0.45	0.17	0.18	−10.0	71.0	0.23	−0.25
0.90	0.49	0.44	0.26	41.0	71.0	0.001	−0.34
0.97	0.49	0.72	0.34	52.0	70.0	−0.08	−0.4
0.99	0.47	1.07	0.45	58.0	68.0	−0.15	−0.45
P90/P10		8.8	1.73				
RD(%)			80.3				
$n_0 = 0.04$	$x_0 = 0.13$	$F_0 = 0.003$					
P90/P50		2.59	1.44				
RD(%)			44.3				

Table A14 Rank Order $u = -\frac{1}{x} - \frac{1}{(1-l)}$

	$\theta = 2.0$		X/Z = 0.9				
F(n)	l	Z	x	ATR%	MTR%	E^u	I
0.10	0.19	0.02	0.15	−100.0	71.0	1.6	−0.16
0.50	0.39	0.14	0.19	−29.0	75.0	0.37	−0.23
0.90	0.46	0.51	0.27	46.0	76.0	0.04	−0.34
0.97	0.47	0.96	0.38	60.0	75.0	−0.09	−0.42
0.99	0.46	1.6	0.56	65.0	68.0	−0.24	−0.51
P90/P10		25.5	1.8				
RD(%)			92.9				
P90/P50		3.64	1.42				
RD(%)			60.5				
$n_0 = 0.06$	$x_0 = 0.15$	$F_0 = 0.03$					

Table A15 $u = (x - 1) - a(x - 1)^2 - (1 - l)^{-1}$, a = 5.0

	$\beta = 0.0$	$\theta = 3.3$	X/Z = 0.9				
F(n)	l	Z	x	ATR%	MTR%	E^u	I
0.10	0.26	0.04	0.05	−10.0	9.0	1.3	−0.06
0.50	0.43	0.16	0.15	5.0	14.0	0.53	−0.09
0.90	0.40	0.36	0.31	14.0	26.0	0.27	−0.14
0.97	0.51	0.55	0.44	20.0	36.0	0.17	−0.20
0.99	0.53	0.76	0.57	25.0	41.0	0.05	−0.27

Table A15 (cont.)

β = 0.0	θ = 3.3	X/Z = 0.9
P90/P10	9.0	6.2
RD(%)		31.1
P90/P5	2.25	2.07
RD(%)		8.0
$n_0 = 0.09$	$x_0 = 0.01$	$F_0 = 0.01$

Table A16 $u = (x - 1) - a(x - 1)^2 - (1 - l)^{-1}$, a = 5.0

β= 1	θ=3.3	X/Z=0.9					
F(n)	l	z	x	ATR%	MTR%	E^u	I
0.10	0.18	0.003	0.06		25.0	2.1	−0.05
0.50	0.35	0.13	0.13	1.0	33.0	0.76	−0.08
0.90	0.46	0.33	0.25	23.0	44.0	0.41	−0.11
0.97	0.50	0.54	0.36	33.0	49.0	0.26	−0.16
0.99	0.53	0.75	0.47	37.0	50.0	0.14	−0.20
P90/P50		2.53	1.92				
RD(%)			24.1				
$n_0 = 0.11$	$x_0 = 0.01$	$F_0 = 0.10$					

Table A17 $u = (x - 1) - a(x - 1)^2 - (1 - l)^{-1}$, a = 5.0

β = 0	θ = 2.5	X/Z = 0.9					
F(n)	l	Z	x	ATR%	MTR%	E^u	I
0.10	0.16	0.03	0.05	−95.0	11.0	2.35	−0.05
0.50	0.40	0.15	0.15	−3.0	20.0	0.60	−0.08
0.90	0.50	0.44	0.35	19.0	39.0	0.27	−0.15
0.97	0.51	0.75	0.52	30.0	50.0	0.13	−0.23
0.99	0.51	1.07	0.67	37.0	54.0	−0.05	−0.36
P90/P10		14.7	7.0				
RD(%)			52.3				
P90/P50		3.14	2.33				
RD(%)			26.0				
$n_0 = 0.10$	$x_0 = 0.03$	$F_0 = 0.04$					

Table A18 $u = (x - 1) - a(x - 1)^2 - (1 - l)^{-1}$, a = 5.0

$\beta = 1.0$	$\theta = 2.5$	X/Z = 0.9					
F(n)	l	Z	x	ATR%	MTR%	E^u	I
0.11	0.08	0.01	0.06	−100.0	25.0	5.3	−0.05
0.50	0.32	0.12	0.13	−14.0	39.0	0.92	−0.07
0.90	0.45	0.40	0.28	30.0	54.0	0.42	−0.12
0.97	0.50	0.70	0.41	41.0	59.0	0.24	−0.17
0.99	0.53	1.09	0.57	48.0	59.0	0.05	−0.27
P90/P11		4.9	2.2				
RD(%)			55.0				
P90/P50		3.33	2.15				
RD(%)			35.5				
$n_0 = 0.12$	$x_0 = 0.055$	$F_0 = 0.06$					

Table A19 $u = (x - 1) - a(x - 1)^2 - (1 - l)^{-1}$

$\beta = 0.0$	$\theta = 2.0$	X/Z = 0.9					
F(n)	l	Z	x	ATR%	MTR%	E^u	I
0.10??	0.05	0.01	0.06	−100.0	13.0	8.8	−0.05
0.50	0.37	0.13	0.16	−19.0	27.0	0.71	−0.08
0.90	0.48	0.52	0.39	26.0	52.0	0.30	−0.16
0.97	0.49	0.99	0.58	42.0	64.0	0.12	−0.27
0.99	0.48	1.49	0.75	49.0	65.0	0.15	−0.44
P90/P10		52.0	6.5				
RD(%)			87.5				
P90/P50		4.0	2.44				
RD(%)			39.0				
$n_0 = 0.10$	$x_0 = 0.054$	$F_0 = 0.08$					

Table A20 $u = (x - 1) - a(x - 1)^2 - (1 - l)^{-1}$, a = 5.0

$\beta = 1.0$	$\theta = 2.0$	X/Z = 0.9					
F(n)	l	z	x	ATR%	MTR%	E^u	I
0.11	0.001	0.0001	0.08	−100	26.0		
0.50	0.28	0.10	0.14	−35	44.0	1.1	−0.07
0.90	0.45	0.49	0.31	36.0	61.0	0.41	−0.13
0.97	0.51	1.01	0.50	50.0	65.0	0.15	−0.22
0.99	0.55	1.66	0.75	55.0	53.0	0.27	−0.48

Table A20 (cont.)

β = 1.0	θ = 2.0	X/Z = 0.9	
P90/P10		4.62	1.78
RD(%)			61.6
P90/P50		4.9	2.21
RD(%)			54.0
$n_0 = 0.13$	$x_0 = 0.075$	$F_0 = 0.11$	

Table A21 Rank Order $u = (x - 1) - a(x - 1)^2 - (1 - l)^{-1}$

	θ = 3.3	X/Z =0.9					
F(n)	l	Z	x	ATR%	MTR%	E^u	I
0.10	0.14	0.03	0.06	−100.0	32.0	3.0	−0.05
0.50	0.32	0.12	0.12	−2.0	40.0	0.92	−0.07
0.90	0.45	0.32	0.23	27.0	47.0	0.45	−0.11
0.97	0.50	0.54	0.35	36.0	50.0	0.27	−0.15
0.99	0.53	0.74	0.44	40.0	50.0	0.16	−0.20
P90/P10		10.7	3.8				
RD(%)			63.9				
P90/P50		2.66	1.91				
RD(%)			28.2				
$n_0 = 0.13$	$x_0 = 0.05$	$F_0 = 0.03$					

Table A22 Rank Order $u = (x - 1) - a(x - 1)^2 - (1 - l)^{-1}$, a = 5.0

	θ = 2.5	X/Z = 0.9					
F(n)	l	z	x	ATR%	MTR%	E^u	I
0.10	0.03	0.01	0.06	−100.0	33.0		
0.50	0.28	0.10 `	0.12	−19.0	46.0	1.11	−0.07
0.90	0.44	0.39	0.26	33.0	56.0	0.44	−0.11
0.97	0.50	0.71	0.40	45.0	59.0	0.24	−0.17
0.99	0.54	1.08	0.55	49.0	58.0	0.06	−0.26
P90/P10		39.0	4.33				
RD(%)			88.9				
P90/P50		3.9	2.2				
RD(%)			44.4				
$n_0 = 0.14$	$x_0 = 0.06$	$F_0 = 0.08$					

Table A23 Rank Order $u = (x - 1) - a(x - 1)^2 - (1 - l)^{-1}$, a = 5.0

k = 2.0	θ = 2.0	X/Z = 0.9					
F(n)	l	Z	x	ATR%	MTR%	E^u	I
0.25	0.13	0.03	0.10	−100.0	44.0	3.2	−0.05
0.50	0.24	0.09	0.13	−50.0	51.0	1.32	−0.07
0.90	0.44	0.47	0.29	38.0	64.0	0.45	−0.12
0.97	0.50	0.99	0.46	53.0	69.0	0.21	−0.20
0.99	0.52	1.56	0.64	59.0	68.0	0.03	−0.33
P90/P50		5.22	2.23				
RD(%)			57.3				
n_0 = 0.16	x_0 = 0.085	F_0 = 0.16					

Table A24 $u = -\frac{1}{(x - v\mu)} - \frac{1}{(1-l)}$

β = 0.0	θ = 3.3	R = 0.1	v = 0.1	μ=0.45			
F(n)	l	z	X	ATR%	MTR%	E^u	I
0.10	0.55	0.10	0.16	−55.0	65.0	0.12	−0.20
0.50	0.59	0.22	0.21	−6.0	58.0	−0.03	−0.25
0.90	0.57	0.41	0.29	30.0	57.0	−0.11	−0.36
0.97	0.54	0.57	0.36	37.0	56.0	−0.15	−0.4
0.99	0.52	0.77	0.45	42.0	53.0	−0.2	−0.45
P90/P10		3.9	1.77				
RD(%)			54.6				
P90/P50		1.86	1.38				
RD(%)			29.2				
F_0 = 0.0			x_0 = 0.13				

Table A25 $u = -\frac{1}{(x - v\mu)} - \frac{1}{(1-l)}$

β = 1.0	θ = 3.3	R = 0.1	v = 0.1	μ = 0.45			
F(n)	l	z	X	ATR%	MTR%	E^u	I
0.10	0.40	0.08	0.16	−100.0	79.0	0.462	−0.17
0.50	0.53	0.20	0.19	2.0	73.0	0.09	−0.24
0.90	0.57	0.41	0.26	37.0	67.0	−0.071	−0.33
0.97	0.55	0.60	0.32	46.0	65.0	−0.13	−0.38
0.99	0.53	0.79	0.39	51.0	64.0	−0.17	−0.42
P90/P10		5.13	1.63				
RD(%)			68.2				
P90/P50		2.05	1.37				
RD(%)			33.3				
F_0 = 0.0			x_0 = 0.15				

Table A26 $u = -\frac{1}{(x-v\mu)} - \frac{1}{(1-l)}$

$\beta = 1.0$	$\theta = 2.5$	$R = 0.1$	$v = 0.1$	$\mu = 0.45$			
F(n)	l	z	x	ATR%	MTR%	E^u	I
0.10	0.46	0.07	0.17	−100.0	68.0	0.29	−0.18
0.50	0.54	0.20	0.21	−5.0	66.0	0.05	−0.26
0.90	0.53	0.47	0.30	36.0	67.0	−0.07	−0.35
0.97	0.51	0.74	0.39	48.0	68.0	−0.14	−0.42
0.99	0.48	1.10	0.50	54.0	67.0	−0.22	−0.49
P(90/10)		6.71	1.76				
RD%			73.8				
P90/P50		2.35	1.43				
RD(%)			39.2				
$F_0 = 0.0$			$x_0 = 0.14$				

Table A27 $u = -\frac{1}{(x-v\mu)} - \frac{1}{(1-l)}$

$\beta = 0.0$	$\theta = 2.0$	$R = 0.1$	$v = 0.1$	$\mu = 0.45$			
F(n)	l	z	x	ATR%	MTR%	E^u	I
0.10	0.36	0.04	0.17	−100.0	68.0	0.58	−0.17
0.50	0.49	0.18	0.22	−19.0	71.0	0.15	−0.25
0.90	0.50	0.55	0.31	42.0	74.0	−0.02	−0.35
0.97	0.47	1.00	0.43	57.0	74.0	−0.10	−0.42
0.99	0.46	1.38	0.53	62.0	73.0	−0.21	−0.50
P(90/10)		13.75	1.82				
RD%			86.8				
P90/P50		3.06	1.41				
RD(%)			53.8				
$F_0 = 0.01$			$x_0 = 0.16$				

Table A28 $u = -\frac{1}{(x-v\mu)} - \frac{1}{(1-l)}$

$\beta = 1.0$	$\theta = 2.0$	$R = 0.1$	$v = 0.1$	$\mu = 0.45$			
F(n)	l	z	x	ATR%	MTR%	E^u	I
0.10	0.22	0.03	0.18	−100.0	77.0	1.4	−0.14
0.50	0.42	0.16	0.20	−29.0	80.0	0.32	−0.22
0.90	0.50	0.55	0.28	49.0	80.0	0.02	−0.32
0.97	0.50	1.02	0.38	63.0	78.0	−0.09	−0.40
0.99	0.49	1.69	0.54	68.0	73.0	−0.22	−0.49

Table A28 (cont.)

$\beta = 1.0$	$\theta = 2.0$	$R = 0.1$	$v = 0.1$	$\mu = 0.45$
P(90/10)	18.33	1.55		
RD%		91.2		
P90/P50	3.44	1.4		
RD(%)		59.2		
F(no) = 0.02		$x_0 = 0.17$		

Table A29 Non-welfarism $u = -\frac{1}{(x-v\mu)} - \frac{1}{(1-l)}$

$\beta = 1.0$	$\theta = 3.3$	$R = 0.1$	$v = 0.1$	$\mu = 0.45$			
F(n)	l	z	x	ATR%	MTR%	E^u	I
0.10	0.34	0.06	0.16	−100.0	84.0	0.67	−0.15
0.50	0.55	0.20	0.19	5.0	72.0	0.07	−0.24
0.90	0.57	0.41	0.26	37.0	66.0	−0.07	−0.33
0.97	0.56	0.60	0.33	46.0	63.0	−0.15	−0.39
0.99	0.55	0.79	0.40	50.0	59.0	−0.207	−0.44
P90/P10		6.83	1.63				
RD(%)			76.0				
P90/P50		2.05	1.37				
RD(%)			33.2				
$F_0 = 0.03$			$x_0 = 0.15$				

Table A30 Non-welfarism $u = -\frac{1}{(x-v\mu)} - \frac{1}{(1-l)}$

$\beta = 1.0$	$\theta = 2.0$	$R = 0.1$	$v = 0.1$	$\mu = 0.45$			
F(n)	l	z	x	ATR%	MTR%	EU	I
0.10	0.03	0.004	0.17	−100.0	86.0	1.4	−0.11
0.50	0.43	0.16	0.20	−24.0	80.0	0.30	−0.21
0.90	0.52	0.56	0.28	50.0	78.0	0.01	−0.33
0.97	0.52	1.06	0.40	62.0	73.0	−0.16	−0.42
0.99	0.53	1.74	0.64	64.0	53.0	−0.36	−0.56
P(90/50)		3.5	1.4				
RD%			60.0				
P90/P50		3.5	1.4				
RD(%)			60.0				
F(no) = 0.04			$x_0 = 0.17$				

Appendix B: The Proof of Formula (32)

Consider an adjustment that slightly raises the marginal tax rate by Δt_k at some income level, k (say, in a small interval from k to $k+dk$), leaving all other marginal tax rates unaltered. This has the following effects. (i) Let $H(k)$ be the distribution function of individuals by income k (which equals ρs and so is endogenous), with density $h(k)$. To the first order the tax paid by everyone whose income is larger than k increases by $\Delta t_k dk$ and these individuals are $(1 - H(k))$ in number, tax revenue increases by $(1 - H(k))\Delta t_k dk$.

(ii) The response to the small tax increase Δt_k of an individual earning k is equal to $\Delta k = -k\varepsilon_k \Delta t_k/(1 - t_k)$. Hence the elasticity of labour income with respect to $(1-t_k)$ is $\varepsilon_k = \frac{\Delta k(1-t_k)}{\Delta t}$. The reduction in income dk implies a reduction in tax revenue equal to $t_k dk$. We assume no income effects here. So we have $-dk\Delta t_k h(k)\varepsilon_k k t_k(1 - t_k)$. (iii) This tax increase also creates a social welfare cost of $-dt_k dk[1 - H(k)]\overline{W}(k)$, where $\overline{W}(k) = \varphi(k)$ is defined as the average social marginal welfare weight for individuals with income above k.

At the optimum these effects must exactly cancel out, so that $dt_k dk(1 - H(k)) - dt_k dk h(k)\varepsilon_k k t_k/(1 - t_k) - dt_k dk[1 - H(k)]\varphi(k) = 0$. Dividing by $dt_k dk$ and rewriting we have formula (32) in the text.

Appendix C

Table C1 Example: Levels of $Gini_{factor}$ and $P90/P50_{factor}$ in fourteen advanced countries from the mid-1980s to the mid-2010s

Country	LIS Wave II around 1985 Gini | P90/P50	LIS Wave IV around 1995 Gini | P90/P50	LIS Wave VI around 2004 Gini | P90/P50	LIS Wave IX around 2013 Gini | P90/P50
Australia	43.7 | 2.16 (1985)*	47.9 | 2.34 (1995)	48.3 | 2.42 (2003)	-
Canada	40.8 | 2.16 (1987)	44.9 | 2.29 (1994)	47.7 | 2.42 (2004)	-
Denmark	41.7 | 1.86 (1987)*	44.7 | 2.02 (1995)*	45.0 | 2.00 (2004)	47.7 | 2.14 (2013)*
Finland	38.9 | 1.89 (1987)*	48.1 | 2.36 (1995)	47.5 | 2.28 (2004)	49.1 | 2.40 (2013)*
France	50.7 | 2.46 (1984)*	49.2 | 2.52 (1994)	48.4 | 2.43 (2005)	-
Germany	44.3 | 2.09 (1984)	46.2 | 2.25 (1994)	50.2 | 2.46 (2004)	52.4 | 2.69 (2013)*
Ireland	51.2 | 2.75 (1987)	49.5 | 2.39 (1995)	50.1 | 2.53 (2004)	-
Italy	42.6 | 2.18 (1986)	47.9 | 2.47 (1995)	50.8 | 2.56 (2004)	50.3 | 2.44 (2014)*
Netherlands	48.0 | 2.24 (1987)*	46.7 | 2.14 (1993)*	46.3 | 2.13 (2004)	48.0 | 2.27 (2013)
Norway	36.6 | 1.86 (1986)*	42.6 | 1.93 (1995)	45.5 | 2.12 (2004)	44.7 | 2.13 (2013)*
Spain	43.5 | 2.25 (1985)	51.0 | 2.71 (1995)	45.4 | 2.39 (2004)	52.9 | 3.18 (2013)
Sweden	43.4 | 2.01 (1987)*	49.8 | 2.39 (1995)	47.0 | 2.19 (2005)	-
United Kingdom	50.8 | 2.57 (1986)	54.3 | 2.78 (1995)	53.3 | 2.76 (2004)	54.4 | 2.93 (2013)
United States	46.2 | 2.47 (1986)	49.1 | 2.66 (1994)	49.3 | 2.74 (2004)	51.5 | 2.95 (2013)

Data source: Luxembourg Income Study (LIS) (2017). Authors' calculations

* This year's observation cannot be used in empirical models of Table 15 due to missing information in other variables.

Table C2 Data: Information and descriptive statistics on data used in models of Table 15. Data spans years 1967–2013 but is unbalanced. Number of countries: 14

variable	description	source	N	min	max	mean
$Gini_{factor}$	Gini coefficient for factor incomes (%)	LIS database (2017)	105	38.30	57.50	47.14
$P90/P50_{factor}$	P90/P50 percentile ratio for factor income	LIS database (2017)	105	1.92	3.58	2.38
RD_{Gini}	relative reduction between factor- and disposable-income Gini (%)	LIS database (2017)	105	23.61	55.62	36.71
$RD_{P90/P50}$	relative reduction between factor- and disposable-income P90/P50 ratio (%)	LIS database (2017)	105	5.52	46.25	20.25
φ	redistributive preference measure using the optimal top tax rate formula: $\varphi = 1-(t\alpha\varepsilon/(1-t))$	Top income tax rates (t) from Piketty, Saez and Stantcheva (2014), OECD (2017), and the Association of Finnish Local and Regional Authorities (2017)[a]; Pareto coefficients (α) calculated from the World Inequality Database (2017); we assume constant elasticity ($\varepsilon = 0.20$).	105	0.05	0.84	0.52

government employment	government employment share (%)	OECD (2017); Eurostat (2017)[b]	105	9.33	33.65	19.15
dependency rate	share of population who are 14 years or under or 65 years or over (%)	OECD (2017)	105	30.30	39.55	33.53
openness	sum of exports and imports relative to GDP (%)	OECD (2017)	105	16.41	190.11	62.71
union density	trade union density (%)	OECD (2017)	105	7.67	83.14	35.06
unemployment	unemployment rate (%)	OECD (2017)	105	1.01	26.19	8.36

[a] Piketty, Saez and Stantcheva's data used for years 1967–2010. The OECD data are used to extend series up to 2013. As an exception, the whole Finnish series has been updated using data from the OECD and the Association of Finnish Local and Regional Authorities.

[b] German government employment data from the year 1995 onwards are from Eurostat.

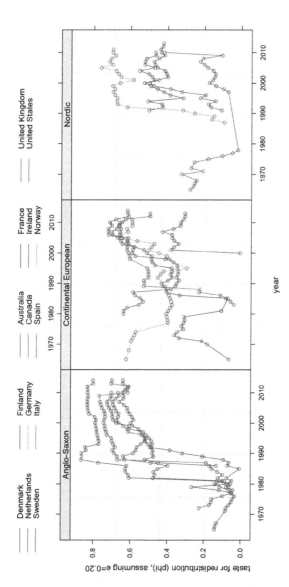

Figure C1 Evolution of the taste of redistribution (φ) in fourteen advanced countries. Authors' calculations based on top income tax rates and Pareto coefficients and assuming constant elasticity ($\varepsilon = 0.20$). See Table C2 for details.

References

Aaberge, R. (2000), Characterizations of Lorenz curves and income distributions, *Social Choice and Welfare* 17, 639–653.

Aaberge, R. and U. Colombino (2006), Designing optimal taxes with a microeconometric model of household labour supply, IZA, DP No. 2468.

Adler, M. (2012), *Well-Being and Fair Distribution: A Framework for Policy Analysis*, Oxford, Oxford University Press.

Ahmad, E. and N. Stern (1984), The theory of reform and Indian indirect taxes, *Journal of Public Economics* 25, 259–298.

Aitchison, J. and J. A. C. Brown (1957), *The Lognormal Distribution*, London, Cambridge University Press.

Alstadsaeter, A. and M. Jacob (2016), Dividend taxes and income shifting, *Scandinavian Journal of Economics* 118(4), 693–717.

Apps, P., N. V. Long and R. Rees (2013), Optimal piecewise linear income taxation, *Journal of Public Economic Theory* 16(4), 523–545.

Aronsson, T. and O. Johansson-Stenman (2008), When the Joneses' consumption hurts: Optimal public good provision and nonlinear income taxation, *Journal of Public Economics* 92, 986–997.

Association of Finnish Local and Regional Authorities (2017).

Atkinson, A. B. (1973), 'La Maxi-Min' et l'Imposition Optimale des Revenus, Cahiers du Séminaire d'Econométrie', 1975, No. 16: 73–86 (French version of University of Essex discussion paper No. 47, January 1973, 'Maxi-Min' and Optimal Income Taxation', accepted for publication by the Review of Economic Studies, but never resubmitted).

Atkinson, A. B. (1990), Public economics and the economic public, *European Economic Review* 34, 225–248 (Presidential Address to the European Economic Association Annual Congress in Augsburg, September 1989).

Atkinson, A. B. (1995), Public economics in action: The basic income/flat tax proposal, Lindahl Lectures, Oxford University Press.

Atkinson, A. B. (1999), Is rising income inequality inevitable? A critique of transatlantic consensus, Wider Annual Lectures 3. Helsinki: UNU-WIDER.

Atkinson, A. B. (2012), The Mirrlees Review and the state of public economics, *Journal of Economic Literature* 50(3), 770–780.

Atkinson, A. B. (2014), Public economics in age of austerity. The Graz Schumpeter Lecture, Routledge.

Atkinson, A. B. and A. Brandolini (2001), Promise and pitfalls in the use of 'secondary' data-sets: Income inequality in OECD countries as a case study, *Journal of Economic Literature* 39(3), 771–799.

Atkinson, A. B. and A. Brandolini (2010), On analyzing the world distribution of income, *World Bank Economic Review* 24(1), 1–37.

Atkinson, A. B. and T. Piketty (eds.) (2010), *Top Incomes: A Global Perspective*, Oxford University Press.

Atkinson, A. B., T. Piketty and E. Saez (2011), Top incomes in the long-run of history, *Journal of Economic Literature* 49(1), 3–71.

Atkinson, A. B. and A. Sandmo (1980), Welfare implications of the taxation of savings, *Economic Journal* 90, 529–549.

Atkinson, A. B. and J. E. Stiglitz (1976), The design of tax structure: Direct versus indirect taxation, *Journal of Public Economics* 6(1–2), 55–75.

Atkinson, A. B. and J. E. Stiglitz (1980), *Lectures in Public Economics*, New York, NY, McGraw Hill.

Banks, J. and P. Diamond (2010), The base for direct taxation, in *Dimensions of Tax Design: The Mirrlees Review*, ed. S. Adam, T. Besley, R. Blundell, S. Bond, R. Chote, M. Gammie, P. Johnson, G. Myles and J. Poterba. Oxford, Oxford University Press, 548–648.

Bargain, O., M. Dolls, D. Neumann, A. Peichl and S. Siegloch (2014), Comparing inequality aversion across countries when labor supply responses differ, *International Tax and Public Finance* 21(5), 845–873.

Bastani, S. and J. Lundberg (2017). Political preferences for redistribution in Sweden, *Journal of Economic Inequality* 15(4), 345–367.

Bastani, S. and D. Waldenström (2018), How should capital be taxed? Theory and evidence from Sweden, CEPR Discussion Papers 12880.

Bernheim, D. G. and A. Rangel (2007), Behavioural public economics: Welfare and policy analysis with non-standard decision makers, in *Behavioural Economics and Its Applications*, ed. P. Diamond and H. Vartiainen, Princeton, NJ, Princeton University Press, 7–84.

Blackorby, C. and D. Donaldson (1988), Cash versus kind, self selection and efficient transfers, *American Economic Review* 78, 691–700.

Blanchflower, D. and A. Oswald (2004), Well-being over time in Britain and the USA, *Journal of Public Economics* 88, 1359–1386.

Blomquist, S. (1993), Interdependent behaviour and the effect of taxes, *Journal of Public Economics*, 51, 211–218.

Blomquist, S. and V. Christiansen (1995), Public provision of private goods as a redistributive device in an optimum income model, *Scandinavian Journal of Economics* 97(4), 547–567.

Blomquist, S. and V. Christiansen (1998), Price subsidies versus public provision, *International Tax and Public Finance* 5(3), 283–306.

Blomquist, S., V. Christiansen and L. Micheletto (2010), Public provision of private goods and nondistortionary marginal tax rates, *American Economic Journal: Economic Policy* 2, 1–27.

Boadway, R. (2012), *From Optimal Tax Theory to Tax Policy: Retrospective and Prospective Views, the 2009 Munich Lectures*, Cambridge, MA, MIT Press.

Boadway, R. and L. Jacquet (2008), Optimal marginal and average income taxation under maximin, *Journal of Economic Theory* 143, 425–441.

Boadway, R. and M. Marchand (1995), The use of public expenditures for redistributive purposes, *Oxford Economic Papers* 47(1), 45–59.

Boadway, R., M. Marchand and M. Sato (1998), Subsidies versus public provision of private goods as instruments for redistribution, *Scandinavian Journal of Economics* 100(39), 545–564.

Boadway R. and M. Sato (2011), Optimal income taxation with uncertain earnings: A synthesis, CESIfo Working Papers 3654, CESIfo Group, Munich.

Boadway, R., M. Marchand, and P. Pestieau (2000), Redistribution with unobservable bequests: A case for taxing capital income, *Scandinavian Journal of Economics* 102(2), 253–267.

Boskin, M. J. and E. Sheshinski (1978), Individual welfare depends upon relative income, *Quarterly Journal of Economics* 92, 589–601.

Bourguignon, F. and A. Spadaro (2012), Tax-benefit revealed social preferences, *Journal of Economic Inequality* 10(1), 75–108.

Bowles, S. and Y. Park (2005), Emulation, inequality, and work hours: Was Thorsten Veblen right?*Economic Journal* 115, F397–F412.

Brett, C. (1997), Notes on non-linear taxation in an OLG model. University of Essex. mimeo.

Chamley, C. (1986), Optimal taxation of capital income in general equilibrium with infinite lives, *Econometrica* 54(3), 607–622.

Champernowne, D. G. (1937), Notes on Income Distribution, Econometrica, Report of Econometric Conference at New College in 1936.

Champernowne, D. G. (1952), The graduation of income distributions, *Econometrica* 20, 591–615.

Champernowne, D. G. and F. A. Cowell (1999), *Economic Inequality and Income Distribution*, Cambridge University Press.

Chetty, R. (2006), A new method of estimating risk aversion, *American Economic Review* 96(5), 1821–1834.

Christiansen, V. (1981), Evaluation of public projects under optimal taxation, *Review of Economic Studies* 48, 447–457.

Christiansen, V. and E. S. Jansen (1978). Implicit social preferences in the Norwegian system of social preferences, *Journal of Public Economics* 10, 217–245.

Christiansen, V. and M. Tuomala (2008), On taxing capital income with income shifting, *International Tax and Public Finance* 15(4), 527–545.

Cowell, F. (1977), *Measuring Inequality*, Oxford University Press, 3rd edn (2011).

Cowell, F. and K. Gardiner (1999), Welfare weights, LSE, mimeo.

Creedy, J. (2009), An approximation for the optimal linear income tax rate, *Australian Economic Papers* 48(3), 224–236.

Cremer, H. and F. Gahvari (1997), In-kind transfers, self-selection and optimal tax policy, *European Economic Review* 41(1), 97–114.

Cremer, H., P. Pestieau and J.-C. Rochet (2003), Capital income taxation when inherited wealth is not observable, *Journal of Public Economics* 87, 2475–2490.

Dahan, M. and M. Strawczynski (2012), Optimal asymptotic income tax rate, *Journal of Public Economic Theory* 14(5), 737–755.

Deininger, K. and L. Squire (1996), A new data set measuring income inequality, *World Bank Economic Review* 10(3), 565–591.

Diamond, P. A. (1965), National debt in a neo-classical growth model, *American Economic Review* 55, 1126–1150.

Diamond, P. A. (1968), Negative taxes and the poverty problem – A review article, *National Tax Journal* 21(3), 288–303.

Diamond, P. A. (1998), Optimal income taxation: An example with a U-shaped pattern of optimal marginal tax rates, *American Economic Review* 88(1), 83–95.

Eaton, J. and H. S. Rosen (1980), Optimal redistributive taxation and uncertainty, *Quarterly Journal of Economics* 95(2), 357–364.

Feldstein,M. (2012), The Mirrlees review, *Journal of Economic Literature* 50(3), 781–790.

Foster, J., J. Greer and E. Thorbecke (1984), A class of decomposable poverty measures, *Econometrica* 52, 761–766.

Gerritsen, A. (2016), Optimal nonlinear taxation: The dual approach. Working Paper of the Max Planck Institute for Tax Law and Public Finance No. 2016–2.

Gruber, J. and E. Saez (2002), The elasticity of taxable income: Evidence and implications, *Journal of Public Economics* 84, 1–32.

Harju, J. and T. Matikka (2016), The elasticity of taxable income and income shifting: What is 'real' and what is not? *International Tax and Public Finance* 23(4), 640–669.

Hsu, M. and C. C. Yang (2013), Optimal linear and two-bracket income taxes with idiosyncratic earnings risk, *Journal of Public Economics* 105, 58–71.

Immervoll, H. and L. Richardson (2011), Redistribution policy and inequality reduction in OECD countries: What has changed in two decades? OECD Social, Employment and Migration Working Papers, No. 122, OECD Publishing. http://dx.doi.org/10.1787/5kg5dlkhjq0x-en (24 January 2016).

Immonen, R., R. Kanbur, M. Keen and M. Tuomala (1998), Tagging and taxing: The optimal use of categorical and income information, *Economica* 65, 179–192.

Ireland, N. (2001), Optimal income tax in the presence of status effects, *Journal of Public Economics* 81, 193–212.

Jacobs, B., E. L. W. Jongen and F. T. Zoutman (2017), Revealed social preferences of Dutch political parties, *Journal of Public Economics* 156, 81–100.

Jäntti, M., M. Riihelä, R. Sullström and M. Tuomala (2010), Trends in top income shares in Finland, in *Top Incomes: A Global Perspective*, ed. A. B. Atkinson and T. Piketty, Oxford, Oxford University Press.

Judd, K. (1985), Redistributive taxation in a simple perfect foresight model, *Journal of Public Economics* 28(1), 59–83.

Kanbur, R., M. Keen and M. Tuomala (1994), Optimal non-linear income taxation for the alleviation of income-poverty, *European Economic Review* 38, 1613–1632.

Kanbur, R., T. Paukkeri, J. Pirttilä and M. Tuomala (2018), Optimal taxation and public provision for poverty minimization, *International Tax and Public Finance* 25(1), 64–98.

Kanbur, R., J. Pirttilä and M. Tuomala (2008), Moral hazard, income taxation and prospect theory, *Scandinavian Journal of Economics* 110(2), 321–337.

Kanbur, R. and M. Tuomala (1994), Inherent inequality and the optimal graduation of marginal tax rates, *Scandinavian Journal of Economics* 96(2), 275–282.

Kanbur, R. and M. Tuomala (2010), Charitable conservatism, poverty radicalism and inequality aversion, *Journal of Economic Inequality* 9(3), 417–431.

Kanbur, R. and M. Tuomala (2013), Relativity, inequality, and optimal non-linear income taxation, *International Economic Review* 54(4), 1199–1217.

Kanbur, R. and M. Tuomala (2014), Groupings and the gains from tagging, Tampere Economic Working Papers, Net Series No. 86, University of Tampere.

Kaplow, L. (2010), Concavity of utility, concavity of welfare, and redistribution of income, *International Tax Public Finance* 17, 25–42.

Keane, M. and R. Moffitt (2001), A structural model of multiple welfare program participation and labor supply, *International Economic Review* 39(3), 553–589.

Kesselman, J. R. and I. Garfinkel (1978), Professor Friedman, meet Lady Rhys-Williams: NIT vs. CIT, *Journal of Public Economics* 10(2), 179–216.

Lindhe, T., J. Södersten and A. Öberg (2002), Economic effects of taxing closed corporations under a dual income tax, *Ifo Studies* 48, 575–610.

Lockwood, B. B., C. Nathanson and E. Glen Weyl (2012), Taxation and the Allocation of Talent. Unpublished.

Lockwood, B. B. and M. Weinzierl (2016), Positive and normative judgments implicit in U.S. tax policy, and the costs of unequal growth and recessions, *Journal of Monetary Economics* 77, 30–47.

Low, H. and D. Maldoom (2004), Optimal taxation, prudence and risk-sharing, *Journal of Public Economics* 88, 443–464.

Mankiw, G. N., M. Weinzierl and D. Yagan (2009), Optimal taxation in theory and practice, *Journal of Economic Perspectives* 23(4), 147–174.

Micheletto, L. (2011), Optimal nonlinear redistributive taxation and public good provision in an economy with Veblen effects, *Journal of Public Economic Theory* 13(1), 71–96.

Mirrlees, J. A. (1971), An exploration in the theory of optimum income taxation, *Review of Economic Studies* 38, 175–208.

Mirrlees, J. A. (1974), Notes on welfare economics, information and uncertainty, in *Essays in Equilibrium Behaviour under Uncertainty*, ed. M. Balch, D. McFadden, and S. Wu, Amsterdam, North-Holland.

Mirrlees, J. A. (1976), Optimal tax theory: A synthesis, *Journal of Public Economics* 6, 327–358.

Mirrlees, J. A. (1990), Taxing uncertain incomes, *Oxford Economic Papers* 42, 34–45.

Naito, H. (1999), Re-examination of uniform commodity taxes under a non-linear income tax system and its implication for production efficiency, *Journal of Public Economics* 71, 165–188.

Nichols, A. L. and R. J. Zeckhauser (1982), Targeting transfers through restrictions on recipients, *American Economic Review* 72, 372–377.

O'Donoghue, T. and M. Rabin (2001), Choice and procrastination, *Quarterly Journal of Economics* 116, 121–160.

O'Donoghue, T. and M. Rabin (2003), Studying optimal paternalism, illustrated by a model of sin taxes, *American Economic Review* 93, 186–191.

Ordover, J. and E. Phelps (1979), The concept of optimal taxation in the overlapping generations model of capital and wealth, *Journal of Public Economics* 2, 1–26.

Oswald, A. (1983), Altruism, jealousy and the theory of optimal nonlinear taxation, *Journal of Public Economics* 20, 77–87.

Pareto, V. (1896), *Cours d'économie politique professé a l'université de Lausanne*, Vol. I 1896, Vol. II 1897.

Parfit, D. (1991), Equality or Priority, Lindley Lecture.

Park, N.-H. (1991), Steady-state solutions of optimal tax mixes in an overlapping generations model, *Journal of Public Economics* 46, 227–246.

Persson, M. and A. Sandmo (2005), Taxation and tournaments, *Journal of Public Economic Theory* 7, 543–559.

Piketty, T. (1997), La redistribution fiscale face au chômage, *Revue française d'économie* 12(1), 157–201.

Piketty, T., E. Saez and S. Stantcheva (2014), Optimal taxation of top labor incomes: A tale of three elasticities, *American Economic Journal: Economic Policy* 6(1), 230–271.

Piketty, T. and G. Zucman (2014), Capital is back: Wealth-income ratios in rich countries 1700–2010, *Quarterly Journal of Economics* 129(3), 1155–1210.

Pirttilä, J. and H. Selin (2011), Income shifting within a dual income tax system: evidence from the Finnish tax reform of 1993, *Scandinavian Journal of Economics* 113(1), 120–144.

Pirttilä, J. and M. Tuomala (2001), On optimal non-linear taxation and public good provision in an overlapping generations economy, *Journal of Public Economics* 79, 485–501.

Pirttilä, J. and M. Tuomala (2002), Publicly provided private goods and redistribution: A general equilibrium approach, *Scandinavian Journal of Economics* 104(1), 173–188.

Pirttilä, J. and M. Tuomala (2004), Poverty alleviation and tax policy. *European Economic Review* 48, 1075–1090.

Pirttilä, J. and M. Tuomala (2005), Public versus private production decisions: Redistribution and the size of the public sector, *FinanzArchiv* 61(1), 120–137.

Pirttilä, J. and M. Tuomala (2007), Labour income uncertainty, taxation and public good provision, *Economic Journal* 117, 567–582.

Rawls, J. (1971), *Theory of Justice.*, Cambridge, MA, Harvard University Press.

Rawls, J. (1974), Some reasons for the maxi-min criterion, *American Economic Review: Papers and Proceedings.*141–146.

Rawls, J. (1982), Social unity and primary goods, in *Utilitarianism and Beyond*, ed. A. Sen and B. Williams, Cambridge University Press, 159–185.

Revesz, J. T. (1989), The optimal taxation of labour income, *Public Finance/ Finances Publiques* 44, 433–475.

Riihelä, M., R. Sullström and M. Tuomala (2007), Varallisuuserot kasvussa, in *Kasvun hedelmät*, ed. H. Taimio, Helsinki, TSL (in Finnish),

Riihelä, M., R. Sullström and M. Tuomala (2014), Top incomes and top tax rates: Implications for optimal taxation of top incomes in Finland, Tampere Economic Working Papers, Net series No. 88, University of Tampere.

Roberts, K. (2000), A reconsideration of optimal income tax, in *Incentives, Organization and Public Economics, Papers in Honour of Sir James Mirrlees*, ed. P. Hammond and G. Myles, Oxford, Oxford University Press.

Rodrik, D. (1998), Why do more open economies have bigger governments? *Journal of Political Economy* 106(5), 997–1032.

Rothschild, C. and F. Scheuer (2014), Optimal Taxation with Rent-Seeking. www.wiwi.uni-frankfurt.de/kolloquium/ws1213_/Scheuer.pdf.

Sadka, E. (1976), On income distribution, incentive effects and optimal income taxation, *Review of Economic Studies* 43(2), 261–267.

Saez, E. (2001), Using elasticities to derive optimal income tax rates, *Review of Economic Studies* 68, 205–229.

Saez, E. and S. Stantcheva (2016), A simpler theory of optimal capital taxation, NBER Working Paper No. 22664.

Sandmo, A. (1983), Ex post welfare economics and the theory of merit goods, *Economica* 50, 19–33.

Seade, J (1980), Optimal non-linear policies for non-utilitarian motives, in *Income Distribution: The Limits to Redistribution*, ed. D. A. Collard, R. Lecomber and M. Slater, Bristol, Scientechnica.

Sen, A. (1974), Informational bases of alternative welfare approaches: Aggregation and income distribution, *Journal of Public Economics* 3(4), 387–403.

Sheshinski, E. (1972), The optimal linear income tax, *Review of Economic Studies* 39(3), 297–302.

Slemrod, J., S. Yitzhaki, J. Mayshar and M. Lundholm (1994), The optimal two-bracket linear income tax, *Journal of Public Economics* 53(2), 269–290.

Stern, N. (1976), On the specification of optimum income taxation, *Journal of Public Economics* 6, 123–162.

Stern, N. (1977), Welfare weights and the elasticity of the marginal valuation of income, in *Studies in Modern Economic Analysis*, ed. M. Artis and R. Nobay, Oxford, Basil Blackwell Publishers.

Stiglitz, J. E. (1987), Pareto-efficient and optimal taxation and the new welfare economics, in *Handbook of Public Economics*, Vol. II, ed. A. Auerbach, and M. Feldstein, Amsterdam, Elsevier.

Straub, L. and I. Werning (2014), Positive long run capital taxation: Chamley-Judd revisited, NBER Working Paper No. 20441.

Tanninen, H. and M. Tuomala (2005), Inherent inequality and the extent of redistribution in OECD Countries. *CESifo DICE Report* 3(1), 48–53.

Tanninen, H. and M. Tuomala (2008), Work hours, inequality and redistribution: Veblen effects reconsidered. Tampere Economic Working Papers, Net Series No. 70, University of Tampere.

Tanninen, H., M. Tuomala and E. Tuominen (2018), Income inequality, redistributive preferences and the extent of redistribution: An empirical application of optimal tax approach. Tampere Economic Working Papers, Net Series No. 124, University of Tampere.

Thoresen, T. O. and A. Alstadsaeter (2010), Shifts in organizational form under a dual income tax system, *FinanzArchiv* 66(4), 384–418.

Tuomala, M. (1979), Optimal Income Taxation and Uncertainty, mimeo, University of Helsinki

Tuomala, M. (1984), Optimal degree of progressivity under income uncertainty, *Scandinavian Journal of Economics* 87, 184–93.

Tuomala, M. (1986), On the optimal income taxation and educational decisions, *Journal of Public Economics* 30, 183–198.

Tuomala, M. (1990), *Optimal Income Tax and Redistribution*, New York, NY, and Oxford, Oxford University Press.

Tuomala, M. (2016), *Optimal Redistributive Taxation*. Oxford, Oxford University Press.

Varian, H. (1980), Redistributive taxation as social insurance, *Journal of Public Economics* 14, 49–68.

Weinzierl, M C. (2012), Why do we redistribute so much but tag so little? The principle of equal sacrifice and optimal taxation, Harvard Business School Working Paper, No. 12–64.

Wilson, R. (1993), *Nonlinear Pricing*. Oxford: Oxford University Press.

Acknowledgements

We are grateful for helpful comments from two reviewers. Funding from the Strategic Research Council (SRC) at the Academy of Finland (project no. 293120, 'Work, Inequality and Public Policy') is gratefully acknowledged.

Cambridge Elements ≡

Public Economics

Robin Boadway

Queen's University

Robin Boadway is Emeritus Professor of Economics at Queen's University.
His main research interests are in public economics, welfare economics and fiscal
federalism.

Frank A. Cowell

The London School of Economics and Political Science

Frank A. Cowell is Professor of Economics at the London School of Economics.
His main research interests are in inequality, mobility and the distribution of income
and wealth.

Massimo Florio

University of Milan

Massimo Florio is Professor of Public Economics at the University of Milan. His main
interests are in cost-benefit analysis, regional policy, privatization, public enterprise,
network industries and the socio-economic impact of research infrastructures.

About the Series

The Cambridge Elements of Public Economics provides authoritative and up-to-date
reviews of core topics and recent developments in the field. It includes state-of-the-art
contributions on all areas in the field. The editors are particularly interested in the new
frontiers of quantitative methods in public economics, experimental approaches,
behavioral public finance, empirical and theoretical analysis of the quality
of government and institutions.

Cambridge Elements ≡

Public Economics

Elements in the Series

Cost–Benefit Analysis
Per-Olav Johansson and Bengt Kriström

Real and Imagined Threats to the Welfare State
Peter H. Lindert

Inequality and Optimal Redistribution
Hannu Tanninen, Matti Tuomala and Elina Tuominen

A full series listing is available at: www.cambridge.org/ElePubEcon

Printed in the United States
By Bookmasters